praise for *wide*

"*Wide Awake: A Buddhist Guide for Teens* is a wonderful expression of Buddhist teaching, in a clear and accessible form. With relevant examples from the teenage perspective, and guided meditations as pragmatic tools, this book powerfully serves the younger community."
—Sharon Salzberg, author of *Faith: Trusting Your Own Deepest Experience*

"Bravo to Diana Winston for a really good, honest book on Buddhism for teens. She's been there and tells how you can do it yourself."
—Jack Kornfield, author of *A Path With Heart*

"Ah, to be young again . . . and have this kind of wisdom available. Diana Winston translates the Buddha's teaching into the language of modern teens, and makes the ancient wisdom relevant to their concerns. A significant contribution to the awakening of the West . . . "
—Wes Nisker, editor of the Buddhist journal *Inquiring Mind*, and author of *Essential Crazy Wisdom* and *Buddha's Nature*

"Diana Winston has given us a great gift—she has offered the heart of the Buddha's teachings for the next generation. Written with grace, wisdom, and honesty, Wide Awake is a wise companion for any teen trying to navigate the tumultuous terrain of the teen and young adult years."
—Soren Gordhamer, author of *Just Say OM!*

"The Buddha instructed his disciples to 'go forth and teach the holy Dharma in the idiom of the people' and Diana Winston is fluent in 'Young Adult.' I think the Buddha would have been proud of her translation."
—Sylvia Boorstein, author of *Pay Attention, For Goodness' Sake: Practicing The Perfections of the Heart*

"Diana Winston writes with astonishing clarity and simplicity about deep spiritual matters. Though *Wide Awake* is a terrific Buddhist guide for young people, I confess that I learned quite a bit from it myself!"
—Norman Fischer, author of *Taking Our Places: The Buddhist Path of Truly Growing Up*

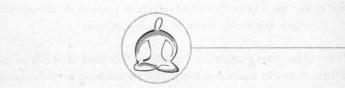

DIANA WINSTON

a perigee book

wide awake

a buddhist guide for teens

P

A Perigee Book
Published by The Berkley Publishing Group
A division of Penguin Group (USA) Inc.
375 Hudson Street
New York, New York 10014

Copyright © 2003 by Diana Winston
Text design by Tiffany Kukec
Cover design by Ben Gibson
Cover photo copyright © Kerwin Roche / Photonica
Author photo by Martin Matzinger

First edition: August 2003

Library of Congress Cataloging-in-Publication Data

Winston, Diana.
    Wide awake : a Buddhist guide for teens / Diana Winston.—
1st. Perigee ed.
        p.   cm.
    "A Perigee book."
    Includes index.
    ISBN 0-399-52897-0
    1. Spiritual life—Buddhism.   2. Compassion—Religious aspects—
Buddhism.   3. Buddhism—Doctrines.   I. Title.

BQ5670 . W46 2003
294.3'44—dc21

                                                2002192666

PRINTED IN THE UNITED STATES OF AMERICA

10   9

contents

contents

appendices

acknowledgments

A book like this is, without a doubt, a collaborative effort, and I have tremendous appreciation for the many people who jumped aboard to offer their support, insights, and enthusiasm.

The highest order of praise goes to Stephany Evans, agent extraordinaire, whose brilliant eye, patient critique, and incredible faith in the project and in me has made *Wide Awake* what it is today.

Much gratitude to Christel Winkler, my editor at Perigee Books, whose excitement for the book was contagious. And to Jennifer Repo, who set the book into motion.

A deep bow to Santikaro Bhikkhu, for sending me to the original texts, debating dhamma points, and offering illuminating feedback and clarification that was never too one-ish.

Profound appreciation to my writing mentors, Barbara Gates and Susan Moon, who provided a forum for my writings, nurtured and helped me develop the craft, and picked me up in difficult times.

Love and gratitude to my collaborators in working with teens: Marv Belzer, Rebecca Bradshaw, Tempel Smith, and other members of the Spirit Rock Teen Teachers' Council and IMS Young Adult's Retreat Helpers. And especially Michele

McDonald-Smith, who nurtured the teen retreat and taught us all how to teach.

Gracias to Ron Applin and Ray Henton for the Costa Rican writing adventure, and to Mesa Refuge for another heavenly writing retreat. Thanks to Paul LeMay for emergency computer assistance every time things went wacko. To Kirsten Mundt for transcription work, and to Dennis Crean for getting me off to a good start.

Appreciation for teens and adults who read chapters and manuscripts, and offered feedback: Adi Bemak for her eye to diversity issues, Dana Becker, Michael Brooks, Arianna Cortesi, Corey Cohen, Kyla Collins, Jeff Denese, Brian Kalish, Josh McFall, Caitlin O'Donnell, Sophie Simon-Ortiz, Galen Rogers, Donald Rothberg, Amy Schmidt, Alan and Silvie Senauke, Heather Sundberg, Aran Watson, Marvin and Isa Winston.

Miscellaneous people who contributed to this work in some way, whether they know it or not, include: James Baraz, Darcy Brown-Martin, Valentino Giacomin, Soren Gordhamer, Sara Hurley, Jack Kornfield, Noah Levine for sending the project my way and gracefully offering his words of wisdom; Maia Duerr and Pam Weiss of the eating/writing group; Nina Wise for tips on muscular writing, Lewis Woods for dhammalogy debate, and everyone at BPF who put up with me during the process.

Love and gratitude to Roni Rogers for unfailing emotional support, kvelling, editing, unconditional approval (no matter what stage of the process she always liked it), wisdom, clothes, and all the things a mother does best. And to Martin Matzinger, who was there in love all the way.

My greatest appreciation is for the teenagers who have taught me so much throughout the years in the Teen Meditation Classes and Young Adult's Retreats, Girl's Dharma Group, and Alice Project School in India. This book would not be here without you. And, of course, it is for you.

Foreword

NOAH LEVINE

As a teen, I searched high and low (mostly high) for some sense of belonging, purpose, and meaning. After many years of a confused quest that led to addiction, violence, and eventually jail, I discovered the simple solution to my crisis in Buddhist meditation practice. In the beginning, at times my meditation practice felt lonely and isolated. It seemed like I was the only young person in the world who was practicing meditation and trying to follow a spiritual path. The books I read were all written by and for middle-aged people. I longed for teachings that were directly applicable to me as a young adult. Eventually I began to meet other people who, like me, had started on the spiritual path at an unusually young age. Diana is one of those people.

Wide Awake: A Buddhist Guide for Teens is the book I was looking for as a teen. In this simple and wise offering of the Buddhist teachings the path of Freedom is clearly and beautifully extended as an open invitation to anyone who is seeking meaning, happiness and a sense of ease. This book shines the light of wisdom into the sometimes dark experience of being young. It lays out the tools necessary to do the work to get through difficult times and help us to awaken to our own natural joy and peace of mind. Diana explains the Buddhist Path of Awakening in a direct and precise manner that is a pleasure to read. She skillfully weaves together teachings from all the major schools of Buddhism, revealing the important questions and answers in a manner that brings about insight, compassion, and illumination of the nature of human life.

As Buddhism is translated from culture to culture and generation to generation, although the teaching remains the same, the way in which it is taught has been constantly changing for over 2,500 years. This book is the culmination of centuries of Wisdom in the East and decades of Buddhism in the West. It is the perfect guide to the perils, pitfalls and mysteries of transitioning into adulthood in an age of so much confusion and misinformation.

The spiritual path goes against the stream, against the system, and at times against our own self-centered desires. Buddhist practice leads to freedom from greed, hatred and delusion. Through meditation, wise action, service and positive intention we can each live the life we long to live. It is a simple path; it just takes commitment and practice. Along the way you will surely discover more than you ever expected—more joy, more love and more freedom.

In Buddhist practice I have found everything that I previously sought in the unskillful and often painful actions of my youth. It is my hope that you will benefit from these words, this book, and these teachings in the same way I have. May you be fortunate enough to want Truth more than anything else and may our paths cross on the journey from here to there.

In service of the truth and defiance of everything else,
Noah Levine and the whole Dharma Punx Posse

introduction: riding the roller coaster

I had no peace
because I didn't know my own mind.
—Sama, a Buddhist nun (from Therigatha)

Why is it that the teenage years can feel like a roller coaster ride? At first the view at the top is great: you can relax, lean back, and coast. You were just asked out by the guy or girl of your dreams; you were awarded the scholarship you were hoping for; and you passed your driver's test—all in one day. Then suddenly, out of the blue, you careen to the bottom of the tracks. Your parents announce they are getting a divorce. Your best friend tells you he or she is moving. You open your eyes, as if for the first time, to the suffering on the planet—as well as in your very own neighborhood—violence, poverty, injustice.

In truth, life for most people, no matter what their age, is filled with continual ups and downs, swings into extremes, happiness and unhappiness. How can anyone ever find safety and security amid these changes?

It seems that constant changes can make life way too stressful. All of you experience, to varying degrees, difficult situations at home—fighting with parents or siblings, the pressures at school—to do well or to even be there at all—competitive social dynamics, and relationship problems. So many of us have minds that are plagued with anxiety and worry.

Meanwhile, difficult choices regularly present themselves. Should you hang out with that crowd you like so much even though they may be seriously involved with drugs? Should you and your girlfriend or boyfriend break up? Should you smoke (anything)? Shoplift? Have sex? Stop having sex?

And the larger "life questions" can plague you: What am I going to do when I finish high school? Am I straight or gay? Will I ever make an impact on the world? And some will be haunted by questions about being alive: What is it all about? Is there a purpose to my life? Really, who am I?

How do we make sense of the roller coaster of the teenage years? Where are the sign posts for life? What maps are there? Who are the mentors? Are there any instruction books? What kind of guidelines are out there to help during these confusing yet certainly wonderful times?

This book, an introduction to the teachings and practices of the Buddha, is written for you, no matter what your experiences or background. Through these teachings and practices you may be able to find a peace and steadiness amid life's turbulent changes. This book may not make your life less stressful, but it might show you another option to relate to life's ups and downs. It will not hand you the answers to your questions, but it will provide you with a framework, and offer tools, suggestions, and practices, so that you can arrive at the answers yourself.

Buddhism offers practices such as meditation, to help us relax, calm down, and concentrate our minds. From this calm, spacious, and quiet mind, we can discover who indeed we really are, free from our conceptions and judgments of how we are supposed to be. In fact, the Buddhist meditation technique, which I will present in the book, is one of the most profound and accessible ways I know for finding answers to those fundamental identity questions.

The age-old wisdom of the Buddha also provides guidelines for making choices, practical advice that makes sense even 2,500 years after the Buddha's death. Buddhist ethical teachings—on values, morals, or how to conduct our lives—can lead to healthier and more harmonious ways of being in the world. In order to benefit from the teachings, we do not have to think of ourselves as "religious" or even "spiritual," although many practicing Buddhists are both of these. The principles of Buddhism may be put into practice at the most mundane level of everyday life. They are of practical use to anyone of any religion, or no religion, of any background, on any path.

You may have picked up this book for a number of reasons. Perhaps you have a specific spiritual question or just a vague spiritual longing. Perhaps you need an answer to a life question. Perhaps you feel as if you have been on that roller coaster a little too long, and are looking for peace and freedom from stress. Or maybe you are not even sure why you picked this book up—you just feel drawn somehow.

The Buddha once said, "Be a lamp unto yourself." This means that, ultimately, you are your own best guide, and can gain truth and understanding by your own efforts alone. But it certainly helps to have a little advice along the path. This book is meant in that spirit.

how did i get started?

I grew up with a hippie mother who was a spiritual seeker. We lived in a conservative New England town, but inside our house we hung pictures of gurus (spiritual teachers) on the walls. We ate tofu, talked about reincarnation, and demonstrated for peace at marches and rallies. My dad more or less put up with it, although spirituality was not his interest at the time. I was embarrassed by my weird upbringing, and felt I would never fit in.

In junior high school I was unsure of the social rules and

didn't have the right clothes or listen to the right music. I found solace in books, studying, and getting good grades. Yet I didn't want to be seen as different from the other kids.

In high school the real pressures began. My classmates and I were told: "You are doing well in school; you can get into a good college; you can get a good job; then you will make a lot of money." It was the 1980s, Ronald Reagan was president, and his administration's financial-security messages were filtering down to sixteen-year-olds. I was not sure I believed this hype, but I wanted to be accepted by the other kids. Drawn into the race, I studied harder than ever, competed for the best grades, and tried to be first in my class.

The success I had worked so hard for came with my acceptance to college. Yet was the prestige and financial security I had been promised really what life was about? I entered college pretty suspicious of this cultural message.

In college I was soon swept away by student activism. I attended sit-ins and demonstrations against nuclear weapons and to protest apartheid in South Africa. I joined the women's political action group and formed a street theater company. I experimented with drugs, alcohol, and sexuality. I wore only black and smoked clove cigarettes. I saw so many of my friends under the spell of materialism, seeking approval, trying to fit into the system, and I knew I wanted no part of that.

I graduated from college unsure about my life and where it would take me. I had criticized the culture, but I also felt part of it. College had not prepared me for real life, that was for sure. I was angry and resentful. What was I supposed to do with my life? I knew making money was not the answer, and I was burned out on activism.

My mother and her spiritual teachers had influenced me enough to consider that the answers to my problems might be found in Asia. So in 1989, I flew to India. Four months later I was living in the Buddhist hill town of Dharamsala and working for a Tibetan rights organization. Each morning I awoke in my cramped hotel room to the sound of bells and chanting and the smell of incense, the mountain, sewage, and urine.

The more I worked for the cause of Tibetan freedom from Chinese rule, the closer I grew to the Tibetan Buddhist culture. A friend suggested I try a Buddhist meditation retreat. I laughed at the idea! I believed myself to be far too political to be spiritual. But as my friendships grew with the Tibetan people, I became intrigued. One day I joined a ten-day study retreat at a little meditation center on the nearby mountaintop.

At first most of it didn't make much sense to me, but one morning at five A.M. as thirty of us huddled together under our shawls in the cramped meditation hall, a short, solemn American nun spoke. She told us that the world will always have opposites, the dualities of pleasure and pain, gain and loss, praise and blame, fame and dishonor. This is the nature of the world; you cannot escape these opposites no matter how hard you try to experience only the pleasant half of each pair. She explained how most of us spend all our time running around after the desirable side, like praise, not accepting the fact that at some point we will also receive blame.

Hearing this was as if I had put on a clean pair of eyeglasses when for twenty-two years I had been looking out through foggy lenses. Her words seemed to explain my life! At last, I thought, someone is telling me the truth about life. I had been running around madly seeking only success and praise. Whenever I did not receive them, I was shattered. Who I was, I realized, was completely dependent upon what others thought of me.

At first, though, I felt hopeless. To hear that everything gained will also be lost was not exactly comforting. But the next part of the nun's teachings blew my mind. This may be the truth of things, she said, but there is a deeper truth. *We can train our minds to find happiness with what is. We can find peace and stability amid all the ups and downs in life.* A much deeper peace is possible. This is the teaching of the Buddha.

After that eye-opening introduction, I then threw myself into years of Buddhist meditation practice and study. I meditated on retreats of many months to deepen my intellectual understanding. I began to experience for myself the potential of a peaceful mind amid changing conditions of life. I spent years in silence, during which I learned who I actually was, even when I didn't want to face it. I even spent a year in Burma (Myanmar) living as a traditional Buddhist nun and practicing meditation in the forest. In 1993, I started teaching Buddhism to teenagers, and I have seen how valuable these teachings have been in helping young people through the confusions and joys of growing up.

This is my story. You have your own. No matter what your story is, finding peace amid changing conditions is available to any of us.

Wide Awake is about the teachings of the Buddha as I have come to understand and experience them. Sometimes I teach directly from the words of the Buddha. Sometimes I offer the interpretation of my teachers or their teachers. And sometimes I offer the teachings in a way that makes sense to me, and I hope makes sense to you. I have also included the thoughts and voices of teenagers I know and have taught over the years; you will find these in italics throughout the book. Most of the names have been changed. There is a glossary in the back that explains foreign words and concepts.

Please remember, you don't have to adopt Buddhism as your religion in order to read this book or do any of the practices, exercises, or reflections I describe. Buddhism is a commonsense and practical philosophy as well as a religion, and it can be practiced by anyone. Many people, whether or not they are Buddhists, find the insights and practices of Buddhism so helpful that they simply apply them to their lives.

The book is divided into five sections, or parts. The first is "Starting Out On Our Journey," key teachings of the Buddha to help you understand the Buddhist way of viewing the world. In the second section, "Learning to Meditate," I will introduce you to the basics of Buddhist meditation and discuss the difficulties and benefits of a meditation practice. The third section, "Surfacing Our Inner Goodness," applies some of the earlier teachings to the difficult issue of self-esteem. This section encourages us to be ourselves, fully. Fourth is "How Do We Live Our Lives?", a section dedicated to help you day-to-day, as you make decisions about issues like your sexuality, mind-altering substances, and communication. The last section, "Out In The World," provides you with some ideas about how you can apply Buddhist teachings to your relations with other people and the planet, as well as how to meaningfully express yourself through your work in the world and make a difference. The book is designed so that it can be read either from cover to cover or at random. You can pick it up when you are in the mood, and go to the chapters that speak most directly to you. It is up to you.

My hope is that this book can serve as a handbook for the roller coaster of the teenage years. I see it as a compass for when we are lost in difficult times, and a companion for wonderful times as well. The book is based on the incredible wisdom of a 2,500-year-old tradition that still has value for us today. I hope this book will be useful to you in whatever you do. Through its teachings, may you be encouraged to always inquire within, access the peace and freedom that is available to you in every moment, and keep moving forward, opening to ever increasing possibilities for happiness on your own path.

May this book benefit all beings!

part one

starting out on our journey

one

who was the buddha?

If you were to ask me, "What is the essence of Buddhism?" I would answer that it's to awaken. And the function of that awakening is learning how to serve.
—Bernard Glassman, contempory Zen teacher

The historical Buddha did not begin his life as some magical awakened being. He started out as an ordinary young man who was actually quite spoiled. But he was intensely curious about the world. More than anything, he wanted to understand why life worked as it did. He was willing even to disobey his parents in order to find the truth. This is his story:

Siddhartha Gautama was born a prince of the Shakya clan in Northern India about 550 B.C.E. When Siddhartha was born, his parents, like other parents during that time, received a prophecy. They were told that their son would have one of two paths in life. Either he would be a great king and ruler, or he would be a mystic and saint. His parents much preferred the idea of a king for a son. So the prince was brought up as a warrior-king, learning the arts of archery and swordsmanship. He learned to win at battle, to strategize, and gain the trust of his men. His parents gave him everything imaginable: lovers, delicious food, jewels, silks, horses.

Siddhartha's parents also sheltered the young prince from "real life." He lived luxuriously behind castle walls and never saw poor people. No old people served in the palace. When the prince and his entourage toured the town, the king's men would police the streets in advance, hiding away the sick, dying, homeless, and insane. For nearly thirty years, the prince never saw nor came in contact with suffering.

Then one day, when he turned twenty-nine, Siddhartha felt a restlessness he couldn't explain. He had a beautiful wife and child, yet his life felt meaningless, empty. He felt disgust for this indolent palace life. There must be more to the world than *stuff*, he thought. (Does this experience feel at all familiar?) So, late one night when the family and servants were asleep, he sneaked out of the palace gates. With his charioteer friend Channa, he entered the city, without illusions for the first time.

According to the legend, the prince encountered four signs. First he nearly tripped over a man in the street who was covered in sores and breathing shallowly. "What's wrong with him?" asked the repulsed Siddhartha.

Channa told him the man was sick.

"*Sick,* what is *sick?*"

"The body is subject to decay and disease. It's not always healthy like yours."

Next they met a woman whose gray hair, missing teeth, wrinkles, and bent-over back baffled the prince.

"Channa, what is *wrong* with this woman?"

"That, my prince, is old age. We all will get old one day."

"Even me?"

"Even you."

Just then they stumbled on a body that wasn't moving.

"Channa, there's no air in this man's lungs."

"Sir, he is dead."

"What is death?"

"Death cannot be escaped. Everyone you know will die, including you."

At that point the prince got depressed. He sat down on the side of the road with his head in his hands.

Now as a side note, is it possible a young man in ancient India had never seen a sick, aged, or dying person? Hardly likely. Although I like the story as it is, I take it as a metaphor: that the truth of the signs had never sunk in until that night on the street. Sometimes we can be told about sickness or death, but it is only when we experience for ourselves that we finally understand it.

As the prince sat there in his despair, suddenly a man with a shaven head, dressed in orange robes, a spiritual seeker of sorts, appeared in his line of vision. He seemed . . . what was it? So . . . peaceful, at home in the world. "Channa, who is *he*?"

"That, my lord, is a mendicant. He has renounced the world to seek the ultimate meaning of all things. He seeks to unlock the mystery of old age, sickness and death."

"I want to do this, too!"

"Your parents won't like it."

Channa's words haunted the prince, and proved correct.

"What do you mean, you're *leaving*?" his father shouted at him.

"I want to understand life. I can't stay cooped up in this castle. Dad, it's all been a lie. Why have you withheld reality from me?"

They wrangled and fought until late into the night, the king pleading that if Siddhartha left it would kill his mother. The prince stood firm.

I imagine Siddhartha felt the worst about leaving his wife and child. This decision has been debated throughout Buddhist history. How could he be so selfish? Would he have become the

Buddha if he stayed with his family? I can't make excuses for the prince, he was doing what he thought he had to do. Later his wife and child also became enlightened. But that, as they say, is another story.

The next morning, Siddhartha left the castle with Channa. He cut off his long, thick hair—the sign of the Shakya clan. He went into the forest, as countless others had done, to find the meaning of this world.

During this period in Indian history, spiritual teachers populated the forest, practically one under every tree. For six years, Siddhartha traveled from one teacher to the next. It is said that he excelled everywhere. In a short time he learned to concentrate his mind so well he surpassed his first teacher. He sought out another teacher of high repute. Again he exceeded his teacher's ability, and again he moved on. Although he learned significant spiritual practices—mysticism, meditations, yoga, fasting, and prayers—not one answered the question of the meaning of life, birth, old age, sickness, and death.

Over time the prince became a celebrity. Soon five wide-eyed disciples followed him from teacher to teacher. Prince Siddhartha was always the best—the best at debating, the most spiritually advanced, the greatest spiritual practitioner among thousands. He worked particularly hard at learning to control his senses by not eating, mistakenly thinking that fasting would bring him enlightenment. At one point he was down to only one grain of rice per day. He was so skinny he could touch his spine by poking his belly. (There are statues of the starving Buddha all over Asia today.)

However, in spite of the training, discipline, teachings, and practices, Siddhartha was not satisfied. He had been practicing for years, and still he felt no closer to the truth. He wondered whether he would die of hunger, failing at his task. "This is really getting me nowhere," he thought. At that moment a young girl named Sujata walked by and offered him a bowl of rice milk. He didn't know if he should eat it. Suddenly a memory appeared before his eyes. He remembered being a young boy sitting in the shade of a rose apple tree while his father worked in the gardens. He felt protected by the tree and experienced a bliss and peace he had never felt before. In that moment he was doing nothing to starve or challenge his body, but something wonderful had happened in his mind.

"Maybe I have gone too far," he thought. "Maybe starvation isn't the way to freedom."

Returning to the present, he accepted Sujata's milk and drank, feeling his body strengthen. His self-righteous disciples were horrified. They accused him of giving up and they went off in search of someone more holy.

In that magical moment when Siddhartha had his childhood vision, he had been sitting under a beautiful pipal tree with heart-shaped leaves. Today it is known as the Bodhi Tree, or tree of awakening, because it became the site of the Buddha's full awakening. He was no longer hungry and could think more clearly. "Let's see," he mused, "Since asceticism didn't work, and no teacher has been able to explain the meaning of life to me, perhaps I need to look within. Could it possibly be inside me?" Then he made a vow:

If the end is attainable by human effort, I will not rest or relax until it is attained. Let only my skin and sinews and bones remain. Let my flesh and blood dry up. I will not stop the course of my effort until I win that which may be won by human ability, human effort, human exertion.

The prince sat under the tree for twenty-four hours. There are many stories about what happened that night. Some may be folklore, some may be true. They say that in the first six hours, Mara—the god of temptation—harassed him. Mara's daughters danced and caressed and tried to seduce the prince. More realistically perhaps, Siddhartha's mind tormented him with memories and fantasies of sexual desire, wonderful foods, and all the worldly pleasures he had left behind. Next, Mara dispatched his armies to defeat the prince. They shot him with arrows, burned his body, and clubbed and beat him. In truth, it is more possible that mind-numbing pain tortured the prince's unmoving body.

Then Mara tried to make him doubt his task: "Who do you think you are to understand the nature of reality? You arrogant, self-centered, spoiled prince, you worthless nothing. You'll never . . ." (Can you relate to this? Have you ever made a vow or determined to accomplish something and had to face doubts that arose to stop you?)

For twelve hours Siddhartha battled his mind. At the height of the combat, when he could take it no more, he reached down and touched the earth. He begged for strength and clarity. Statues throughout the Buddhist world immortalize this gesture: "Calling Earth to Witness." The earth came to his rescue and offered him her strength. He did not give up.

In the final six hours, what is called the last "watch of the night," Siddhartha finally got it. A veil lifted and he saw into the world from beginningless to endless time. He understood the origin of the universe, and how we are reborn. He uncovered what is called "dependent origination," or how the suffering that binds us to the cycle of birth and death is created. He understood how to get free of this cycle. He entered into this freedom and, as they say, "went beyond," and touched *nirvana*— the unconditioned, unborn, deathless. Prince Siddhartha became enlightened and from that moment on was known as the Buddha, or the Awakened One.

Siddhartha basked in the truth for seven days. He considered permanently hiding out in the forest—after all, how would anyone now be able to understand him? But a god named Brahma Sahampati persuaded him to teach. For although most people were confused, there were a few whose "eyes were only partially covered with dust," and might be able to hear and follow his teachings. Brahma assured him that if people learned of the Buddha's discovery, they too could walk the path and discover freedom for themselves.

The Buddha began a forty-five-year career as the leading spiritual teacher of his time. During his lifetime, he wandered from village to village, through towns and cities, resting only for three months during the rainy season. He taught exactly what he had discovered for himself, and he led thousands of people to reach the same insights he had attained. His teachings are called the *dharma*—which means "teachings" or "truths" that lead to harmony in life.

An order of monks became his followers, and later an order of nuns formed, too. He had many students from all backgrounds. He taught kings and queens, merchants and servants, the rich and the poor, and even children. He preached wisdom, love, and compassion to all who asked. He offered a set of practices that encompassed the development of generosity, renunciation, ethics, wisdom, and meditation.

The Buddha was not interested in teaching a lot of theory. He said, "I teach one thing and one thing only, suffering and the end of suffering." He was not interested in speculations such as where the universe comes from and why we were born. He cared about human suffering, and how that suffering could come to an end. He did not say that God would liberate us or intervene to help us. In fact, there is no deity in Buddhism. Instead he talked about the power of human ability, human skill, and human perseverance. Each of us could find our own freedom from suffering in this life if we made the effort.

The Buddhist texts are filled with stories of his teaching, and the ways that countless lives were transformed by it. Some stories are of a mystical nature. Others are more down to earth. In all cases, the Buddha uncompromisingly advocated clear insight, skillful action, and an end to suffering.

then what happened?

Though Siddhartha was not childless, when he died at eighty-five, he left no spiritual heir. He often said that each of us must be our own guide, our own true teacher. The teachings of the Buddha were memorized by his followers and were not written down until five hundred years after his death. You can certainly imagine that his words were subject to interpretation, and anyone might claim they possessed the true teaching of the Buddha. In fact, at one point there were eighteen schools of Buddhism, each claiming that they taught the real thing!

The many schools of Buddhism spread throughout Asia over two thousand years. Followers brought them from ancient India (where the Buddha's teaching later died out) down to Sri Lanka, Southeast Asia—Thailand, Burma, Cambodia, Laos, and Indonesia, then north to China, Tibet, Korea, and Japan. Within each country also arose great masters and teachers, following the steps of the Buddha, but forming their own schools and lineages.

Wherever the teachings flourished, they mixed with local culture and tradition so that each country had its own unique Buddhist flavor. The practices and teachings differ outwardly from one another, although they are similar in essence. For instance, in Japanese Pure Land Buddhism, followers chant about the heavenly realm and hope to be reborn there. Whereas, in Thai forest monasticism, some Buddhist monks live in caves and practice silent meditation for years at a time.

The Buddha didn't call his teachings "Buddhism." In the nineteenth century, European scholars labeled the religion practiced

wide awake .

throughout most of Asia "Buddhism." I will use the term Buddhism for convenience's sake, since that is how we commonly know this spiritual and religious movement. Today, approximately 500 million people all over the planet call themselves Buddhist. It is the world's fourth largest religion.

Eventually Buddhism came to Europe and North America. First, Asian immigration brought the whole range of Buddhist practices to the developed world. Immigrants started their own temples and practices on the foreign soil and often taught anyone who was interested. Europeans and Americans traveled to Asia, early in the nineteenth century and then later in the twentieth century, especially during the 1950s, 1960s, and 1970s. In the 1950s, the Beat poets of San Francisco and New York (like Jack Kerouac and Alan Ginsburg) were introduced to Japanese Zen Buddhist teachings, and their writing exhibits that Zen influence. A decade later, the hippies and spiritual seekers flew or backpacked overland to India and Thailand, lived for years in monasteries and temples and practiced with great masters. They brought back to their home countries the sacred teachings and practices that they had learned from masters all throughout Asia. The seekers in turn started their own meditation centers and temples.

My own teachers, Joseph Goldstein, Sharon Salzberg, Jack Kornfield, and others traveled to Thailand, Burma, and India, some lived as monks and nuns in the 1970s, and came back and taught the practice of insight meditation, which I learned in the 1980s.

Currently in my city of Berkeley, California, we can find a Japanese-influenced American Zen Buddhist temple on the same block as a Thai temple where Thai Buddhist monks live. We have several different kinds of Tibetan centers, a Japanese Buddhist university, a nearby American insight meditation retreat center, and a Chinese Buddhist monastery.

*   *   *

When I reflect on the Buddha's life, I am amazed by his story. One young man chose to step outside his parent's expectations and to look deeply inside himself. His discoveries would affect millions of people for more than two thousand years!

two

trust your direct experience: the kalama sutta

Make an island of yourself,

make yourself your refuge;

there is no other refuge.

Make truth your island,

make truth your refuge;

there is no other refuge.

—the Buddha

There are two kinds of faith. One is a kind of blind trust in the Buddha, the teachings, the master, which often leads one to practice. The second is true faith—certain, unshakeable—which arises from knowing within oneself.

—Ajahn Chah, Thai Buddhist Master

The first time I looked at a map of India, I got dizzy. The country is vast, crammed with different religions, sub-cultures, and ethnic groups. I was positive that in every village, on every mountaintop, and in every temple, there was sure to live a holy man or woman—a guru, a teacher, a wise person who might have The Answer. I dreamed of traveling to India to meet one of these masters, but truthfully, I was intimidated. I didn't know where to start. I didn't know who to listen to or if I should chant, pray, meditate, or shave my head. I had imagined and heard about so many teachers, all who seemed to have "supreme knowledge." How would I know which path to follow or whom to believe? This question is an ancient one, and has been the challenge of every spiritual seeker, no matter their age or the age in which they live.

More than 2,500 years ago during the lifetime of the Buddha, people in Northern India were asking themselves the same questions. At that time, according to the stories, the forests were filled with spiritual teachers. Seekers huddled beneath trees to listen to all kinds of holy men preach.

But every teacher offered different advice. Some spoke of bathing in the Ganges River to purify the mind. Others suggested fasting for months. Still others proclaimed that since cows were holy, if one walked on all fours and mooed, one could reach enlightenment. Except in some obvious cases, the people could not easily discriminate among these teachings.

The Kalama people, who lived in a small village, were baffled by the variety of teachings and could not decide whom or what to believe. One day they heard that a man known as "the recluse Gautama" (the Buddha) was coming into town. He was greatly admired as one supreme in knowledge, self-awakened. He also had a reputation for being good at answering questions.

When the Buddha arrived in the village, the Kalama people swarmed around him. "Sir," they asked, "many holy men stop by our village and say their teachings are the best and others are nonsense. Then another teacher shows up and says, 'Don't listen to that guy!' We have heard so many different teachings that we are *very* confused. We don't know to whom we should listen or what we should believe."

The Buddha paused for a moment, scratched his chin and replied: "I can understand how confusing this is. Of course you are uncertain, of course you are in doubt. Here is my advice: <u>Neither</u>

believe nor reject anything simply because you have heard it. Do not believe in traditions simply because they have been handed down for generations. Do not believe what is written in religious books. Do not believe something just because it superficially seems to be true. Do not believe something for reasons of logic or philosophy. Do not believe anything merely by authority of your teachers and elders. Even if *I* tell you something, do not believe it!"

"Great. Then what *do* we do?" the Kalamas asked.

The Buddha responded: "When you know for yourself that a thing leads to harm for yourself and others, and is blamed by people who are wise, do not follow it. When you know for

kalama sutta in a nutshell

Do not believe something because:

- you have heard it before

- it is an old tradition

- it is written in religious or other books

- superficially it seems true

- logically or philosophically it seems to be true

- teachers or elders say it is true (even famous ones)

Only believe something you have clearly seen for yourself to be true. If after fully examining, experiencing, and carefully considering a teaching or some advice, and you find that it leads to happiness for one and all, accept it and live up to it.

yourself that a thing is good, is praised by people who are wise, and leads to benefit and happiness, follow it." This advice, one of the most basic principles of Buddhism, is known at the _Kalama Sutta_ ("sutta" means "teaching" and is pronounced as "soo-ta").

The Buddha encouraged people to fully examine, experience, and consider teachings and advice carefully. He suggested that _only when you can verify a teaching by your own direct experience_—by seeing its positive results in your life—then and only then, should you believe it and act accordingly. The Buddha asked people not to forget their own intelligence and wisdom.

trying out the advice

Luckily I didn't let my fears stop me from travelling to India. I did travel to the country, I met a number of impressive gurus, sat at the feet of reputable masters, and studied Indian philosophies. Ultimately I began a Buddhist practice in the town of Dharamsala, in Northern India. Because the teachings seemed to match so closely with my direct experience, I had to search no further. However, within Buddhism itself, I had a lot of questions. I soon found I was able to apply the wisdom of the Kalama Sutta to my study of Buddhist teachings.

Early on, I heard about two teachings. One was about rebirth. The other concerned "clinging." The first teaching made no sense to me. How can I know whether or not there is rebirth? I mean, I don't remember what happened before I was born. How could I accept something I did not have direct experience with (did not see its results in my life)? It sounded important to Buddhism and it interested me, but I wanted to let it sit, brew inside me, and wait to see how it would fit in as I learned more. I chose not to accept the teaching right away.

The teachings on clinging, or _attachment_ were another story. When I learned that the Buddha had said that suffering is rooted in attachment, I began to seriously contemplate and consider this teaching. I looked at how it played out in my life. I made a list of all the things I was attached to: people, material objects, pleasant experiences, and then some intangibles like praise, good grades, and being liked. I saw for myself that if I didn't get them, I suffered. If I lost any of them, I suffered. I was attached to having these things. I put far more weight on them than they deserved. My whole identity was tied up in getting the "good" stuff and escaping the "bad."

After spending months looking at attachments in my life, I realized, the Buddha was right! I had applied the principles of the Kalama Sutta to this new Buddhist teaching. I rigorously questioned and examined the teaching until I understood it with my direct experience and saw that following it led to more happiness.

questioning is healthy

The Kalama Sutta made a lot of sense to me. But after a while I began to worry that by following the guidelines of the Kalama Sutta, I would question *everything*. Yet skepticism has an undeserved negative reputation. Actually, I discovered, questioning is healthy.

During that same time in Dharamsala, I had a friend who was an American Buddhist monk. Most of the Buddhists I met were older than I was, but Paul was twenty-five so we had a lot in common to talk about. We used to sit on the side of the road drinking *chai,* the milky tea that is always too deliciously sweet. We talked about hitchhiking, about our favorite musicians, and we also talked about the *dharma*: the teachings of the Buddha for living a harmonious life. I had a million questions, of course, and I was getting what seemed like textbook answers from my Buddhist teachers. But Paul always was able to make me understand.

One sunny day on a grassy slope of a mountainside, I said to him, "All these teachings are incredible, but Paul, I don't necessarily believe everything! I mean, how do I know what to accept? I'm worried that I'm questioning it all too much. Maybe I'm too critical."

His eyes gleamed. "Diana," he said, "questioning is the best way to learn something new, particularly a spiritual path. Keep checking it out. Don't assume it's true right away."

"Yeah, but I feel so skeptical. I want to believe it, but some of it seems dogmatic or strange. I don't think I'm approaching it in the right way."

"No way! You are absolutely right. If you do take on these teachings as part of your life, you will have looked at them more carefully than someone who accepts them unquestioningly. They'll be inside you in a real and solid way. They won't be overturned. They'll be yours."

Questioning is an absolutely necessary part of the spiritual journey. It prevents us from "blind faith," or believing something without any verification—what the Buddha warned against in the Kalama Sutta.

weighing the teachings like gold

Echoing the Buddha in the Kalama Sutta, Paul continued, "Accepting Buddhist teachings as truth is like purchasing gold jewelry. If you go to a store to buy a ring, you don't buy any old gold-colored ring. It could be fake. Instead, you pick it up and look at it carefully in good light, you have it weighed and measured, you look for impurities. You might bring it to an expert to ask for a second opinion. Only later, if you are sure it is genuine gold, do you buy the ring."

Spiritual and philosophical teachings require the same scrutiny. You have to check them out first. Try them on like with a new outfit, and see how you feel. Weigh them against what you already consider to be truth. What values and beliefs do you hold most deeply in your life, and where do they come from? How does this new teaching fit in with them? What happens when you act from that belief? Does this teacher's advice lead to getting in trouble or to finding peace, to suffering or to happiness?

the role of a teacher

You may be wondering if Buddhism is about trusting your own experience, what is the role of a teacher on this path? Are teachers important? How do we choose them? Should we even bother with them at all?

Having a teacher varies in importance depending on who you talk to. In some Buddhist traditions, like Zen, the relationship between a teacher and his or her student is intimate and necessary for realization. In Tibetan Buddhism, the teacher is also extremely significant, and one must spend years in practices that honor and develop trust in the teacher. In Southeast Asian monasteries, the teacher is someone who can guide one to deep liberating insight.

In my practice, insight meditation in the United States, teachers are seen more commonly as spiritual guides who help us along the path. We are encouraged to remember that it is the *dharma* (or teachings), not the teacher, who has contributed to our awakening. However, I (like most Buddhists I know) have tremendous gratitude for the teachers who have helped me over the years, such as Joseph Goldstein, Michele McDonald-Smith, Sayadaw U Pandita, Thich Nhat Hanh, Tsoknyi Rinpoche, Ajahn Amaro, Joanna Macy, Maylie Scott, and Valentino Giacomin, among others.

No matter what Buddhist tradition you may feel drawn to, teachers can offer wisdom, explain and instruct us in practices, discuss life questions, and help us to develop along our spiritual path. Teachers are very useful in pointing out where we have gotten stuck.

In fact, although anyone can learn from a book, I recommend that, ultimately, you seek out a teacher, whether someone to whom you have a strong devotional relationship, or just a spiritual friend. If you want to learn guitar, you can start practicing from a book, but after time, if you want to understand the complexities of the instrument and increase your skill, you should seek out a guitar teacher. We can certainly learn about Buddhism on our own, but most of us get to a point when it helps to have some expert guidance.

I recommend that you approach finding a teacher in the way we have explored in this chapter, check them out thoroughly, weighing them like gold! Find out as much as you can about this person, even, if you can, how they behave when they are not teaching. Some wise people say you should work with a teacher for ten years before you say that they are your teacher. Be careful about an impulse that some people have to find a teacher and automatically stop trusting themselves, letting the teacher dictate what they do and think.

When you find a teacher who seems valuable and can help you with your practice, maintain a healthy skepticism, and continue to refer back to your own experience. Weigh their words and actions against what you know to be important and meaningful for you. Never lose sight of your own best judgment.

working with this book

I invite you to approach this book and the Buddhist teachings from the same frame of mind the Buddha encouraged in the Kalama people. You are holding a guidebook that you can consider, explore, argue with, refer back to, study, examine, and weigh against your own experience. Please do it with a sense of exploration. In this book, you will encounter Buddhist teachings filtered through my eyes. Do not, by any means, assume what I have written is truth. Do not accept certain ideas or principles because they are Buddhist and Buddhism is "in."

I am not here to tell you what to believe. Accept any words I have written only if and when they make sense to you on a deep level and you know they lead to happiness. Believe them when some part inside you sighs and says, "Yes, I know for myself, that is true."

exercise your beliefs

Reflect on these questions:

* ❋ What spiritual or religious beliefs do you already hold that are important to you?

* ❋ Where did these beliefs come from?

* ❋ How do you know them to be true?

three

what is being awake?

A brahmin (an Indian holy man) once asked
Buddha, the Blessed One:

"Are you a God?"

"No, brahmin," said The Blessed One.

"Are you a saint?"

"No, brahmin," said The Blessed One.

"Are you a magician?"

"No, brahmin," said The Blessed One.

"What are you then?"

"I am awake."

—Buddhist Legend

My friend Stephanie told me about the first time she went on a silent meditation retreat of ten days. She awoke each morning and practiced being aware of her breath and body, as best she could for the full day. Although her mind seemed to jump around non-stop at first, after a while it became very focused and still.

At six P.M., the meditation center served a light meal, usually of fruit and tea. One evening she chose an orange from the big glass bowl, sat down on the grass outside, and prepared to eat. She peeled the orange with the utmost care and tenderness, feeling the juices squirting onto her fingers, noticing with curiosity and pleasure all the white stringy bits. It was as if nothing in the world existed except her and the orange. The smell was so intense, she thought, like the smell of one hundred oranges. She noticed a pleasurable, anticipatory feeling in her mind. When she finally put the orange section in her mouth and bit down onto it, it was the sweetest, most varied, and most alive taste she had ever experienced. She told me it was the first time she had ever really eaten an orange.

In that moment, Stephanie was truly awake.

Being awake is accessible to all of us. It means being fully present to our lives. A meditation retreat, as in Stephanie's case, can bring out this feeling of being alive, but no retreat is necessary in order for us to wake up. Waking up can happen at any moment, in any place, and can be done by anyone. Yet most of us are not awake in our lives, in fact we have been conditioned to be the opposite, conditioned to space out.

spacing out

Where was your mind most of the day today? Can you even remember how you got from where you were a few hours ago to where you are right now reading this book? Probably not.

Why is it that something so recent should be completely lost to our memory? Because most of us, most of the time, are spacing out.

What we call "spacing out" is a trancelike operating mode. Our focus is internal rather than external and it can seem as though we are not focused on anything at all; we are in a complete stupor. This happens in classes that we find boring or irrelevant, or in the midst of habitual activity—brushing our teeth, eating lunch, or cleaning our room, it can even happen when we are listening to our friend's problems! We simply stop following the action in the scene around us and withdraw our consciousness until someone or something snaps us out of it, bringing our awareness back to the present moment.

This spacing out is often like watching TV in our mind. When we space out, our minds tend to go to one of two places: the past or the future. That is, we spend our present moment either "reliving" or "pre-living." When we relive stories and past events we replay wonderful memories—that fantastic party from last weekend, or our first (or fiftieth!) kiss. But sometimes we spend hours lost in painful memories, reexperiencing how bad we felt, or imagining different outcomes or how we might have done things differently, like seventeen-year-old Graham's experience after a breakup:

> *The other day in math class, all I could think about was Anna breaking up with me. She called me up and said, "Yo, it's over." I said, "Wait, can we talk about this?" And she said no. So my mind kept obsessing how I should have treated her . . . if things could have been different . . . I completely forgot about algebra till my teacher called on me.*

Our minds also hang out in the future. Fifteen-years-old Jia's recollection illustrates how we can spend hours designing a future that is not present, yet seems so vivid:

> *I wanted to get on the volleyball team and I thought for sure I'd make it. Then my mind imagined I would be chosen captain, then MVP, then that our team would win the tournament, especially against the school that always beats us, and then . . . I hadn't actually even made the team yet. It was weird. I do that all the time.*

Worry is another kind of "preliving" way of spacing out. Spacing out isn't always pleasant. Many of us are all too familiar with anxiety about the future. *What if my parents find out about . . . ? I should have studied harder. Will I finish high school? Will I get into the college I want? What if I'm pregnant?* And so on endlessly, until we have tied ourselves up in knots. Worry can cause a lot of suffering—ironically over things that have not yet, and may never, happen!

Spacing out is a protective ability that we probably learned when we were very young. When humans experience too much pain—physical or emotional—one natural reaction of the mind is to dissociate, that is, to let our mind separate from the body, from this place and time, the present moment. In truth, this capacity is very helpful as it prevents us from hurting too badly. The problem is, however, that spacing out has become habitual, overused. We space out not only in extreme situations to avoid pain, but virtually any time that our attention is not absolutely grabbed. It has become more like our normal way of being.

So what? If our life is boring or painful at times, then why not space out? Why not go to sleep and wait for the next amazing experience or the next movie that will entertain us? What is the big deal with spacing out? Well, the big deal is that we are missing the now, when truly, now is all there is. The bottom line is we are missing our lives.

waking up

In order not to just "go through the motions" of living, acting like a spaced-out zombie, we can learn to wake up. Being awake means being fully engaged. When we are awake, we are aware, present, connected, alive in our bodies, attentive in our hearts and minds.

Try to remember a time when you felt like you were really aware of living your life. Maybe it was when you took a walk in the woods with your best friend, or a time when you were completely absorbed in drawing or in writing a song, or when you were running that mile and your body and mind felt in sync. At that time, you were there, with your whole heart and mind. There was nothing in the world that needed to be different than it was, no detail that you would change, even if you had the power to do so. Amelia, who is sixteen, described her trip to the mountains:

> I went camping with my best friend, who's older than me, and it was an amazing experience. She took me out way into the mountains and we were alone in nature and we walked ten miles a day up really steep cliffs. I felt so strong, and so my body felt so alive. It was one of the happiest times of my life.

Of course Amelia was describing what was for her a peak experience, something unusual, profound, and special—situations that "bring us to life," in a way. Imagine if life could be like that a lot, or even most, of the time. The Buddha teaches that by fully waking up to each moment we can learn to be awake and alive in ordinary life. Then ordinary life becomes something extraordinary.

When we are fully conscious, our minds open up to something larger than ourselves. We are no longer caught in our ordinary views, judgments, and concepts. Our usual sense of ourselves disappears. These moments are not generally exciting, but more peaceful and subtle. We usually take them for granted, because most of us crave excitement. But in that moment, we have found peace and freedom. We have woken up. How amazing!

Cultivating self-awareness is a revolutionary act. Everything in our modern world teaches us to be distracted. Contemporary society invites us to be busy, preoccupied, seeking highs and excitement, running from activity to activity. This thrill-seeking becomes addictive, yet the highs may never fully satisfy us—there is always another imagined thrill just around the corner. "Just now" is never enough. We are not conditioned to be quiet or to slow down, and we are certainly not given lessons in how

to be aware. Most of us don't know how to pay more than superficial attention. That is why being awake is so radical and goes
against the culture. The funny thing is, it is so simple.

being in our bodies

The first time I saw the Vietnamese Zen master Thich Nhat Hanh
walk across a grassy field, I was stopped in my tracks. He was
walking like no one I had ever seen before. He didn't seem to be
doing anything overtly unusual; the difference was more subtle.
Hanh walked as if he had nothing else in the world to do except
walk. He walked as if each step was his last step. When he placed
his bare foot down on the lawn, it was as if the earth walked with
him, the grass flattened for him, and a stillness surrounded him.

We can practice being awake in a very simple way, just by
bringing our awareness into our bodies. When we sit, we can
know that our body is sitting. When we eat, we know we are
eating. When we run, we can feel the sensations of the body
running. It is as easy as that—feeling our body, living in it, being
a full human, rather than a head with a body dangling from it.

When Thich Nhat Hanh talks about his ability to be aware, he
says, "There are two ways to wash dishes. The first is to wash
dishes in order to have clean dishes, and the second is to wash the
dishes." If we do our ordinary activities in a spaced-out fashion,
trying to hurry up and do the dishes so we can get to the next
video game, TV program, or bag of potato chips, we are skipping
out, missing our lives. If we engage in our ordinary activities by
paying attention with a fullness of heart and mind, we are awake.
We can perform activities without wishing that the activity would
be any different than it actually is. The process becomes as important as the goal. Being awake is when we are fully there in our
body, noticing all its sensations in this moment, doing an act for
no other reason than to do it. Sujeeta, who is fourteen, experimented with the practice of being aware of her body:

I decided to walk to the bus while noticing how many steps I could be aware of before I spaced out. I left my house and started walking and felt eight steps before I wondered if I had shut the lights off in my house. Then I remembered my game, and became aware of the steps, this time only three steps with my foot crunching the gravel before I was lost in some thought. Then I got really determined to notice my feet stepping, and I counted twenty steps. It was fun. I felt more centered by the time I got to the bus.

knowing our minds

As we learn to be aware of our bodies, we can also develop an understanding of our minds, especially our thoughts and emotions. We can learn what makes us tick: our habits, likes and dislikes, what makes us happy and unhappy, how we react, and what we care about. This understanding is called self-awareness, a quality of mind that is developed simply by paying attention.

Usually thoughts run through our mind without our giving them much attention. Yet they are the key to understanding ourselves. To begin to develop wisdom we need to take a look inside our heads. What do we believe in? What do we think about when we wake up in the middle of the night? What do we fear? Who are we, really?

If, for example, we are thinking about a cute guy or girl, and we are paying attention to our thoughts, we will know that we are thinking. At the same time, we will be aware of *what* we are thinking: "I never noticed him before, how strange . . ." We will deliberately be witnessing our thoughts.

Knowing our thoughts teaches us who we are, and gives us the possibility to make change, as fifteen-year-old Warren found:

I have been trying to practice more awareness of what I think. I listen to myself more, try to notice what my thoughts say. Well, do you know how many times in one day I use the word "can't"? I must think I can't do anything! I never realized how much I handicap myself.

Like Warren, we can learn to recognize the repetitive thoughts that harm us—"I'll always be left out" or "I'll never finish school," and learn to cultivate thinking that is beneficial: "I'm actually an okay person," or "I want to be more true to myself." The more we practice being attentive and aware of our thinking, the more awake we will be.

We can also gain insight into ourselves through noticing our emotions. For example, when we are angry, we will be aware that we are angry. We can explore the roots of our anger, how anger feels, what is useful about it, and what is harming about it. We won't avoid the feeling or try to smother or dull it with excessive eating or TV-watching, or pretending things are okay when they really are not. We will learn to feel the full range of our emotions, without judging them as negative or unallowable. We will see what we are made up of, what makes us alive.

Self-awareness is not judgmental. Self-awareness means we have delved into the mystery of our minds, and have explored all corners of our thoughts and feelings. No thought or emotion is excluded or considered not a part of us. I am not suggesting that we *act* on all our thoughts and emotions. What I am saying, is that we fully get to know ourselves, to become conscious human beings.

"what's that about?"—knowing our motivations and acting from clarity

Another important part of the process of waking up is examining our motivation before we act "unconsciously." Most of the time we have very little awareness of why we do things. We may not be sure why we got involved in a particular relationship, why we dropped out of school, or why we continue to work so hard in school. Usually we act out of habit—because we have been told we are supposed to do something or because we have "always" done it that way. The more we can get in touch with our motivations, the more likely it is that we will act in ways that are in harmony with our deepest values.

Let's take lying as an example. Lies often pop out of our mouths without much forethought. If we were practicing becoming aware of our motivations, and we noticed that we were about to lie, we might ask ourselves, "What's that about? Why do I need to lie?" The answer might interest us—we want attention; we are afraid of hurting or disappointing someone; we are too lazy to tell the truth. Who knows what we will discover. The kinds of motivations we might have in any given situation are very complex, and exploring them serves two purposes. First, we learn more about who we really are, and second, when we understand what our action is all about, we may choose to act differently (not lie in this case). Patricia, who is nineteen, was working with observing her motivations:

I think I used to be pretty unconscious. Now I try to pay close attention to what motivates me. Like when I'm dating a guy, do I put on a certain outfit to please him or to please myself? What's my motivation when I say yes to sex? Is it because I really want to do it, or is it because I don't want him to think I'm not in love with him? I can't believe how much there is to see inside myself when I pay attention to why I do things.

Self awareness implies not only that we *know* who we are, and what we believe in, but also that we take responsibility for *acting* from that knowledge. I have found that when I don't know myself too well, when I don't pay attention to my motivations, I

have hurt myself or others. I am not awake, and my actions are
those of a sleepwalker. For example, had we considered our
motivations, would we have slept with that person? Or would
we have "borrowed" the answers to that test? Or would we still
have spoken so harshly to our sister? *What was that about?* As we
become aware of our motivations, we have more opportunity to
choose how to act. We can bring our behavior in line with our
deepest integrity, acting the way we really wish we could.

the fruits of being awake

Knowing ourselves takes time and work. Truthfully, it is much
easier and convenient to escape into spacing out. However, as
we wake up to our lives, we will find that extraordinary benefits
come from the simple act of paying attention.

The more we are awake and conscious, the more life takes
on a richness we may never have imagined possible. We may feel
more connected to our bodies. The world may seem brighter,
more vivid, more real. We will feel emotions more fully, or
truly appreciate life. Our friends may notice it, too. One day we
will be fully present when listening to a friend's problems.
"Wow," she might say, "You're one of the best listeners I know.
Thanks, it really helped me." We will know ourselves as powerful and competent to care for ourselves, others, and the world.

Waking up is the difference between living life like robots—
dulling out, going to sleep, avoiding reality—and engaging in
the world and being fully human. If you saw the movie *The Ma-
trix*, it is the difference between the red pill and the blue pill.
One pill perpetuates the illusion and keeps us asleep; the other
awakens us to the truth of who we are.

Ultimately, self-awareness is the forerunner of wisdom. The
more we understand ourselves, the wiser we will be. Wisdom
comes from seeing clearly, and waking up is all about seeing ourselves and the world clearly—exactly as it is. Carrie, who is six-

teen revealed how her own inner wisdom developed from waking up to her life through the practice of meditation:

> Before I started meditating I was pretty much like a zombie. I just did what kids are supposed to do, went to school, babysat my little sister, studied, went to swim team. I never realized how much I hated myself. Then when I began to meditate and practice awareness, I was completely shocked at all the ridiculous things my mind said to me, telling me I was too fat, not good enough in school, ugly. Meditation

waking up is . . .

- Consciously and fully engaging with our life

- Being in our bodies—alive and present in this moment

- Appreciating the process as much as the goal

- Experiencing the full richness of the world around us

- Developing self-awareness: knowing what is really going on in our minds and hearts

- Learning more about who we are, cultivating insight and wisdom

- Having a clearer sense of our motivations and acting from that clarity

- Bringing our actions more in harmony with our deepest values

- Of benefit to ourselves, our relationships, and the world

full awakening: nirvana

In Buddhism we talk about the potential of becoming enlightened, or of *fully* waking up. What does this mean?

In the Buddhist tradition, the Sanskrit word nirvana is used to mean a state of full awakening. The word literally means "coolness," and is associated with peace and freedom. Nirvana is seen as the ultimate goal of Buddhism—what the Buddha achieved under the Bodhi Tree.

However, many misconceptions surround the words nirvana and enlightenment. Some people imagine: "If I reach enlightenment, the world will explode into white light," or "I will become one with God," or "I will have omniscience and know how to help all beings on the planet." Or "If I reach nirvana all my problems will be solved," or "I will be extremely powerful and loved."

Some schools of Buddhism say every time we have a moment of awakening, like those moments of self-awareness we explored throughout the chapter, when we are fully present here and now, we are having a "little nirvana." In that case, to reach nirvana, all we have to do is practice waking up in our lives as much as possible for a moment at a time. The late Thai master Ajahn Buddhadasa, who coined the phrase "little nirvana," said,

> *Nirvana* can be present here and now by taking your breath in cool and letting it out cool. It is the realm that cools down the heat, quenches the thirst, and extinguishes the sufferings existing in our daily life—automatically without us being conscious of it. It really is a nourishing process for our life all the time.

As enlightenment ripens, these moments of coolness string themselves together and we wake up for longer and longer periods of time.

Another Buddhist school considers nirvana to be the eradication of three mental "weeds"—greed, hatred, and delusion. These nasty plants "grow" in our minds, and, upon enlightenment, are ripped out at their roots and can never grow again. In their place, generosity, love, and wisdom thrive. They say that the plant is uprooted in stages, a little at a time; more like weeding a garden over the seasons, for many years.

Still other schools of Buddhism say that in truth we are already enlightened, it is our true nature, but we have forgotten. Often this existing enlightenment is called our Buddha-nature—the whole, radiant, inner self that cannot be changed by anything external. In some traditions, our minds are compared to the vast, blue sky, extending as far as the eye can see. However, at times clouds and rainstorms pass by and cover up our true nature. The Zen master Hakuin said, "Although there are countless teachings that instruct us how to obtain enlightenment, the ultimate instruction is there is simply no teaching that is superior to the true practice of the awakening to one's own nature."

How do we make sense of these seemingly contradictory teachings? If I am already enlightened, then why do any spiritual practice? Or if I have a lot of work to do to free my mind from greed, hatred, and delusion, then how could I be already enlightened? These are great questions!

I like to hold the views together. On one hand, I diligently practice meditation and waking up in my daily life, while remembering the incredible human potential of full awakening. Imagine, one day my mind may be completely free from all greed, hatred, and delusion! As I practice, I get more and more tastes of a free mind.

On the other hand, as I develop on my spiritual path, I remember that an awakened heart and mind is true human nature, how can it be otherwise? I try to accept myself exactly as I am. I remind myself that even if I don't *feel* enlightened, being awake is the natural condition of my mind, which I can experience from time to time, and through practice, increasingly more often. Whatever I encounter on my path, no matter how challenging, cannot possibly cover up the pure radiance of my heart.

For some, nirvana means being awake to all of life in entirely new ways. For others, it is the highest ideal of the human heart. Still others see it as fundamentally who we already are. We can remember all these definitions of nirvana, and in the meantime, begin exactly where we are: Taking one step at a time on the path towards being wide awake.

exercise your senses

✳ Eat an orange very slowly with as much awareness as you can. Peel it carefully, observe it fully. Smell it, touch it all over. Put it into your mouth and notice all the tastes. Chew one bite many times. See what you can observe.

✳ The next time you are talking with a friend, try to notice what you are thinking. Are you imagining what will be served for lunch, or worrying about the test you just took? Just notice what is happening in your mind. Don't judge what is happening as good or bad. Then see if you can bring your attention only to your friend's words. Can you fully listen? How is the experience of listening fully and consciously different from the half-listening we often do?

✳ You can try this same experiment with anything else you do—taking a walk, washing your hair, brushing your teeth. What does it feel like to be fully alive and awake in your experience, whatever it is?

four

dropping the banana:
the four noble truths

The Four Noble Truths encompass the entire teaching of the Buddha, just as the footprint of an elephant can encompass the footprints of all other footed beings on earth.

—Ven. Sariputta, the Buddha's chief disciple

Nothing whatsoever should be clung to as I or mine.
—the Buddha

In Thailand, hunters have a special trap to catch monkeys. The hunters hollow out the shell of a good sized coconut and put a ripe banana inside. A monkey's hand is small enough to reach inside the opening of the shell, but too big to come out holding the banana. The hungry monkey reaches in, grasps the banana, and discovers he is caught! He screams and cries, trying desperately to escape this trap. And of course he could, quite easily, but in most cases, the monkey doesn't want to let go of the banana. So he is swiftly captured by the hunters.

We shouldn't feel smug about the monkey missing the obvious solution. Humans are a lot like that ourselves. We hold on firmly to something that keeps us stuck in some hurt or problem. All we have to do is let go, but we don't understand this. So we keep holding on tightly. We can imitate the mon-

key and stay stuck, or simply, we can let go of the banana and
be free.

This story illustrates one of the most important teachings of the Buddha: the Four Noble Truths. Soon after he became enlightened, the Buddha searched out his five followers who had earlier abandoned him when he relaxed his extreme ascetic discipline. He told them that now he had discovered the answers that he had been seeking. In a deer park in Sarnath, India, the Buddha taught the Four Noble Truths to these former disciples.

The Four Truths explain that suffering exists, why it exists, how it can come to an end, and the path one must travel to bring suffering to an end.

This teaching is the very foundation of Buddhism.

first noble truth: there is suffering in life

The Buddha taught the First Noble Truth—the truth that suffering exists in the world. Suffering is a translation of the word *dukkha* (duke-ah) from Pali (rhymes with holly) the language of the early Buddhist texts. Other translations are anguish, unsatisfactoriness, pain, hurt, and stress. The monkey is caught in the trap and is suffering. He is experiencing fear, anxiety and maybe even agony, all of which are dukkha. He may have been in some physical pain, but the main problem was emotional and psychological pain—true dukkha.

Humans suffer any time our lives run contrary to our desires for ourselves, those we love, or for the world. Obvious dukkha includes the pain, shame, disappointment, and sadness we feel when screwing up on the job, getting sick before the big date, falling for the wrong person . . . the list is endless. When we experience any of this emotional pain, we are experiencing the first truth of dukkha. Sometimes even things we usually consider

1. There is suffering in life.

2. Suffering always has causes.

3. An end to the suffering is possible by ending the causes.

4. The Noble Eightfold Path is the way to end suffering.

*The word noble, when used here, literally means beyond the reach of the internal enemies that disturb our lives. So these truths can lead us to safety from enemies.

"good" are actually suffering. For instance, a new relationship or job usually comes with a high level of emotional discomfort.

We may also experience suffering not only within our own lives, but when others are in distress. For example it can be agonizing for us if a friend has an eating disorder, or a relative gets sick with an incurable disease, or maybe even dies, or a close friend overdoses. My friend Amy related this story that happened when she was sixteen:

I came home from school late one December afternoon and my mom was asleep on the bed with what I thought was one of her usual migraines. I went downstairs to do my homework. Two hours later I heard a crash and ran upstairs. I found my mother unconscious on the floor. It was suicide— she had overdosed on four bottles full of pills. Her body was convulsing and her face was blue. I called an ambulance, but it was too late.

I sat there holding her head in my lap in disbelief and to-tal shock. She died in my arms. I kept thinking, "This can't be happening," and I wanted to scream "Why can't someone do something?" I felt despair, anger: How could this be? It was like waking up in a nightmare. I couldn't understand it. A mother can't die!

The ambulance drove off into the cold, snowy night. There was no siren, just the eerie, red ambulance light bouncing off the snowbank. I had a feeling of complete aloneness. Everything was turned upsidedown. We never got to say goodbye.

Maybe, like fourteen-year-old Alice, we suffer when we witness inequality or deprivation elsewhere on the planet—that billions of people live under extreme conditions of war, disease, or poverty:

My parents took me to the Dominican Republic and we stayed at a fancy hotel. One day my mom took my brother and me for a walk and after about a mile the green grass just ended and we were in a shanty town with hundreds of people living in shacks with tin roofs. I had never seen such poverty and was shocked how sheltered I had been all my life. I felt ashamed for my privileged life, and horri-fied by the conditions they lived under. I cried the whole next day.

The Buddha also spoke about the suffering of change. He said that nothing in life is permanent. Things are constantly changing in life, moving from agreeable to disagreeable and back again. We don't understand this, so when life changes, we have stress, we suffer. We will experience the pain of change if our family moves, or if we move from one foster family to another, or if we fall in love, or break off from a relationship. Even the things that presently seem wonderful will change. And no matter what we do, at some point change will come as we experience the suffering of sickness and death.

Because of the uncertainty of life, that is, the fact that life is always changing, many of us feel a sense of dissatisfaction—either a vague or acute sense that things are not quite right. We may feel this even if we do not have obvious suffering in our lives, in fact life may seem pretty good. This is another form of dukkha, the ordinary dissatisfaction that is part of being alive, part of simply existing. Have you ever experienced this existential kind of dukkha?

Hearing about the First Noble Truth made a big difference in my life. As a teenager I experienced the pain of my parent's divorce and relationship woes. After graduating from college without a clear plan for my life, I went through a depression. I also felt a lot of anger, shame, and horror when I perceived injustice in the world. Yet all around me in the media and from adults, was the message that life is supposed to be fine and suffering is not right, *not* okay. Dissatisfaction and pain were problems that should be kept under wraps.

In the developed world people live in denial about suffering. Old people are hidden in elder-care facilities, the sick are secluded in hospitals. The media glorifies happiness, health, wealth, youth, and power, and we can feel like something is wrong with us if we are unhappy, sick, not privileged, or dealing with pain in our lives.

When I first heard the truth of dukkha, I breathed a sigh of relief. Inside I felt a calmness and sense that I could relax. The Buddha was pointing to how things really are. He was teaching it is a mistake to deny reality or to try to cover up the truth of things. At last, someone is acknowledging what I know with my own two eyes and heart—that suffering exists. Ironically, acknowledging the truth of suffering is a powerful act of accepting life. It is full of hope because if we are willing to acknowledge suffering, then we can find a way out of it. Many people hear, "Life is suffering," and think, *Oh,*

is not pessimistic, it is realistic. Besides, the Buddha didn't leave us
hanging with only the First Noble Truth.

second noble truth: suffering always has causes

The Second Noble Truth explains what makes us suffer. This Noble Truth is about the cause of suffering. The origin of suffering
is craving and getting stuck in that craving. The monkey wrapped
his hand around the banana because he craves the banana. But so
long as he holds on tightly (or clings) to the banana, he is trapped,
and alas, suffers. He is completely stuck on, or attached to, the
image of himself possessing the banana. Of course, if he stopped
grasping so tightly to the banana, he could free his hand and
would no longer be trapped. The second noble truth explains that
his clinging onto to the banana is causing him to suffer.

Most of us crave and desire all sorts of pleasurable things of
the world: material objects—cars, new clothes, money, a certain pair of sneakers, and so on. We also crave people—
boyfriends or girlfriends, a popular crowd and the attention
they give us. We want our life to be filled with only happy
events and interesting people. The Buddha referred to this kind
of craving as craving for sense pleasures, anything we can experience through our five senses—eyes, ears, nose, mouth, or
tactile senses—or that which we can imagine experiencing with
our mind.

The Buddha spoke about two other kinds of cravings. The
first is the craving for what we might call "being" or "having." Being is the craving "to be" something. We might want to be a
dancer, musician, a driver, a success in the world, the funniest
person we know, or anything else. Or, in the case of the craving, "to have": We desire to have, for example, praise, recognition, convenience, or ease in our life. We also want to have

interesting experiences; nobody likes to be bored. We seek new thrills that will entertain us, make us happy.

The Buddha also talked about the craving for oblivion—for "*not* being." How often have we desired a deep sleep where we can forget about all our problems? One of the reasons that drugs and alcohol are so popular is because they help numb us for a time, they distance us from our daily anxieties and larger struggles.

Now, it is perfectly normal to have desires or to crave things. The Buddha said that everyone experiences desires for pleasures in the world, for being and having, and for oblivion. The objects of desire are only a small part of the problem. The real problem arises when we get *stuck* on the things that we want, in a way, when they possess *us*! If we want something really badly and we don't get that thing, we suffer. If we do get them and they don't meet our expectations, we are disappointed. Or sometimes our satisfaction is momentary; the thrill passes, like with gifts the day *after* our birthday. We continue to wish it were still our birthday.

We can crave all sorts of things, but when we become attached, we are deluded into thinking something can belong to us or that we could control it. Of course things can belong to us in a temporary way, we all own things. Having possessions is not the problem to which the Buddha was referring. The Buddha was speaking in the larger sense—that everything in the world is constantly changing, and because of how fleeting things are, there is nothing we truly can possess or have full control over. Greg, who is eighteen, experienced this truth of the world:

At the beginning of senior year, Jan and I were the perfect couple. We got along so great. We even planned to go to the same college. I thought I had found my soulmate. We belonged to each other, in a way. Then over the summer I don't know what happened, she started to call me less, said she needed time for herself. Out of the blue she started seeing

*someone else. It was the hardest time in my life, ever, I mean,
I thought we were fated, meant to be together forever.*

When we become attached to our desires or cravings, our sense of who we are becomes dependent upon them. So for instance, if you meet an attractive guy or girl and suddenly begin fantasizing: "This is the one for me." You may either create an entire life-story with this person, or imagine how good it will feel if and when you finally go to bed together. Implicit in the wanting is a *me* who needs the object of our desire. You have locked onto the object, gotten attached, and in doing so have stirred up the "somebody" who needs the object to be happy. You may have thoughts such as "If this person doesn't fall for me too, I will die!" That is attachment.

Of course you may be wondering, how can I still have meaning, purpose, and enjoyment in my life without being stuck in desire? Well, you can have "wise wants" and not be fixated or stuck. A wise want is based in what is beneficial and healthy, but if it is not what is happening right now, or the desire doesn't work out, you will still survive.

In this example, if you see an attractive person and notice your desire for that person, but don't feel like your happiness is dependent upon that person, you are not attached to that craving. It doesn't possess you. You haven't created an identity based on the need to get the object. You can simply notice an interesting, desirable person and think, I would love to be sexual or in a relationship with him or her. At that point you are free to pursue the relationship, but can learn to recognize when you have gotten attached. You can when you have gotten unrealistic about this person providing you with happiness. And if the relationship doesn't work out, your whole life isn't ruined. The truth is, the less clinging, the less your life is ruined.

Working with desire and attachment is something you can explore over your lifetime. You don't have to drop your craving tomorrow. Begin by getting a basic understanding of these noble truths and then see how they work in your own life.

third noble truth: an end to suffering is possible by ending the causes

The Buddha said, "The third noble truth is the complete cessation of that very craving, giving it up, renouncing it, emancipation from it, nonattachment to it." We can have the happiness that comes from not being attached, from letting go of our craving and allowing it to end. This is the Third Noble Truth of the cessation of suffering, where we replace ignorance with wisdom.

In the case of the monkey, if he were to realize that he was caught because of holding onto the banana, and then were to let go of it, he would experience the benefits of the insight of the Third Noble Truth. He would get free and his suffering would end.

The Third Noble Truth tells us *We don't need anything outside of ourselves to be happy* or, *attachment will not lead to happiness.* Happiness is something that comes from the inside. And it comes to us most strongly when we practice letting go, when we cultivate inner peace. It comes to us when we fully experience what is happening in each moment with as much awareness as possible, not wanting it to be different than it is. Satisfaction arises when we regard each moment of beauty lightly, knowing that this experience will too pass or change. The poet William Blake said, "He who binds to himself a joy/Does the winged life destroy;/But he who kisses the joy as it flies/Lives in eternity's sun rise." When we understand the truth of cessation, we begin to recognize our desires, without necessarily habitually acting from them or impulsively following them. The resulting inner peace is the subject of the next chapter.

Miguel, who is twenty-one years old, and began meditating in Juvenile Hall when he was seventeen, explained it this way:

Before I started meditating, my life was all about trying to impress people. I wanted material things, things that were making me more miserable, but I didn't know it. I would do something illegal, then take the money and spend $3,200 to get a Rolex and I'd have it, and then I'd be like, so what? I made myself feel like "Mr. Extravagant." But I had this non-stop paranoia that if I didn't have material things, then I was no one without them. And the truth was, when I got these things I found I wasn't getting acknowledged, and that actually no one cared.

Now I don't get my self-esteem from objects, instead I get it from my practice. Why? Because meditation brings other aspects of my life into harmony—my body and emotions, and then everything runs smoothly. I get my happiness from inside myself, and practice is the key to my happiness. Sure, sometimes I go back to the way I was, going out to buy things to make me happy, but its more like a cycle now, you go back and then up and down, hopefully not too far down, and you keep improving.

The ultimate cessation that the Buddha talked about is called nirvana, which we discussed in an earlier chapter. It means coolness or an extinguishing, like fuel no longer feeding a flame. The fires of our greed, hatred, and delusion have gone out. Whenever we can let go of attachment to a person or object or mental state, we experience a coolness or a calm. Nirvana is a subtle concept, but it is practically accessible here and now. All we have to do is let go. We may experience a delight in the coolness, a sense of relief, a lightness that comes from truly letting go of the grasping. The monkey would feel this relief as he releases the banana and pulls his hand swiftly from the trap—what ease and delight!

Sound easy? Well, as we will discover, letting go is the work of a lifetime. At the same time, each step can be joyful as we let go. But what exactly are these steps? What kind of path can we follow? How can we possibly drop the banana?

the fourth noble truth: the noble eightfold path is the end to suffering

We can now move on to the beauty of the Fourth Noble Truth. In the first truth, the Buddha explains the problem. In the second he explains the cause; in the third the potential resolution; and in the fourth he offers a pathway. If we follow that pathway, we will find freedom from dukkha. If the monkey had been following the Path, he never would have gotten stuck in the trap in the first place!

The Fourth Noble Truth is actually an eight-point prescription for a healthy spiritual life style. The Buddha called it the Eightfold Path, or the Middle Way between extremes. Each point of the Noble Eightfold Path focuses on a particular kind of "right" action, behavior, or attitude. When we hear the word right, we may think that if we are not following the path then we are wrong. And then we may get down on ourselves, judge ourselves, or feel guilty for being imperfect.

I like to think of the word "right" in the Buddhist context as "that which leads to freedom from suffering." The word "wrong" would then be "that which perpetuates or leads to more suffering." Right speech, for example, would be speech that is skillful—leads to harmony and prevents suffering, like truthful and meaningful speech. Wrong speech would be speech that creates more suffering, such as lies or harsh speech. Implicit in this teaching is that happiness comes from becoming a wiser, more skillful, more *harmonious* human being.

Throughout the book I will talk about different aspects of the Eightfold Path. I will offer the Buddhist wisdom teachings to help us learn more about Right View and Right Intention; I will

the noble eightfold path, or the middle way

1. Right View—knowing the truth of suffering, that freedom from suffering is possible, and how to live a life without suffering

2. Right Intention—intending to wake up and help others

3. Right Speech—speaking in harmonious ways and avoiding hurting through speech

4. Right Action—acting in harmonious ways and avoiding hurting through actions

5. Right Livelihood—finding work that is useful, meaningful, nonharming, and expresses who we are in the world

6. Right Effort—putting our beliefs and understanding wholeheartedly into practice

7. Right Mindfulness—paying careful attention to what is happening in our lives

8. Right Concentration—inner stability and calm that allows us to focus on what is helpful for ourselves and others

explain meditation practices for waking up and developing Right Effort, Right Mindfulness and Right Concentration; and I will offer guidelines for how to live in the world in a healthy way: Right Speech, Right Action, and Right Livelihood. As we experiment with living and working in accord with the principles of the Middle Way, we will discover that it is possible to let go of our clinging to our particular bananas, and that we can experience true happiness and true freedom from suffering.

exercise: working with your attachments

※ Make a list of the things that you feel attached to or stuck on in these categories:

- Material possessions

- People

- Experiences

- Identities (e.g., soccer player, grandson, actress . . . or good-looking, unattractive, smart, dumb, pimply, good-complexioned, etc.)

※ Now go back and see if you can notice *how* you get stuck on something. What kind of emotions get stirred up when you think of these objects? For example, can you notice when you have expectations for a particular experience, and disappointment when it doesn't work out.

five

mosquitoes, equanimity, and the eight worldly conditions

> Develop the mind of equilibrium. You will always be
> getting praise and blame, but do not let either affect
> the poise of the mind: follow the calmness, the ab-
> sence of pride.
>
> —Sutta Nipata 702, Buddhist text

The jungles in Burma are brimming with innumerable insects and reptiles. When I spent a year meditating there
as a Buddhist nun, I saw giant spiders the size of my
hand and huge beetles that looked like windup toys. I was particularly revolted by a kind of lizard that looks like a snake with
legs. Life in a Burmese monastery was, at least in part, a daily
study in how not to be grossed out or frightened by the endless
parade of creatures. But believe it or not, I had the most difficulty coping with ordinary mosquitoes.

My meditation hut had holes in the walls. I was told they
were for ventilation, but I knew that really they were intended
to give the mosquitoes a direct route to my flesh. Every evening
at dusk my room filled with a cloud of mosquitoes. I would slide
under my mosquito net and pray no mosquito had also gotten inside to turn my safety net into a torture chamber. I was miserable from the constant itching.

Since my Buddhist vows forbade my killing anything, I spent a lot of time and energy devising ways of getting rid of mosquitoes. I tried putting a bucket filled with stagnant lake water in the room in hopes that the mosquitoes would be drawn to it and I could catch them the next morning. They always escaped. I blocked all the holes in the roof with magazines, but then I got too hot. I even figured out how to stand in front of my window and, as they raced to bite me, I jumped out of the way and they flew out the window. That worked to a degree, but if the wind blew the wrong direction, they would charge straight for me.

Finally, after many months, something occurred to me. I could hide, repair holes, and invent traps, but no matter what I did, there would always be another mosquito. I would never get rid of them for good.

But maybe there was another way. Maybe I could learn to live *with* them. Or, maybe I could learn to let go of wanting to live *without* them, and find a peace and balance *with* the mosquitoes. My happiness could depend on my mind better than on whether or not a mosquito was in my room. "There's always another mosquito" became my secret chant. I had begun to develop equanimity.

Equanimity is a word we don't often use in this country—not surprising since we live in a culture that is in many ways the opposite of equanimity—dramatic, anxious, and filled with extremes. Equanimity is about balance and even-mindedness. *It is a state of mind that is imperturbable.*

The first time I experienced equanimity during meditation practice, I found it startlingly sweet. It was beyond any ordinary feeling of pleasure or excitement that I had ever experienced. My mind felt open and spacious, and at the same time, strong and ready for anything. I was in a true state of balance. Had anyone said I was stupid, I would not have been even slightly disturbed; had anyone said I was brilliant, again, my mind would not have been moved.

Anyone has the potential to find equanimity within, whether or not they meditate. It is simply a state of balanced mind, calm and even in the face of difficulties. Have you ever, for example, received bad news, and rather than scream, cry, or freak out you felt a calm and strength, like, "I can handle this. It will be tough, but I'll manage." If so, you had equanimity, an extraordinary mental quality of peace and strength.

If you have equanimity, you can see benefits directly in your life. If, for instance, you move to a new neighborhood or start a new school, it will be challenging, but with equanimity you will have reserves of calm and even-mindedness to count on. If you have to cope with your parents' divorce or the breakup of your own relationship, with equanimity, you will have the ability to weather the storms. If someone you love is ill, because your mind is balanced you will be more available to help them. Even small irritations in life seem less of a problem thanks to equanimity. An annoying sibling, a fight with a parent, and bad days will all seem less difficult in the light of equanimity.

anicca: the truth of change

One of the most famous teachings of the Buddha is known as the truth of change. In Pali, the language of early Buddhism, we say *anicca* (a-NEE-cha). It means "impermanence." Obviously, everything in the world is changing. The clock ticks forward. Cities are built and eventually crumble. The weather changes with the seasons. Fashions and trends go in cycles.

Nor does anything inside us stay the same from moment to moment. Our bodies grow and age, our cells die off and are re-placed, our moods swing, our thoughts, attitudes, plans, emo-tions . . . everything changes!

While we all say we believe in change, most of us don't live our lives as if this were so. We live as if we believe that everything is supposed to stay the same. When things do change, often we are shocked. We can't believe a pimple would show up right before the big date, or that we could lose our academic standing in school, or that someone we love could leave us or even die.

When I am immersed in an exciting novel, having a delicious meal, or engaging in a great conversation with friends, a voice in me says, "I wish this would last forever." It never does, of course. When I am having a bad day, fighting with a good friend, or worrying about my future, an internal voice says, "things will *never* change, they will *always* be terrible." Again, that is impossible. Like most people, I often live as if I don't believe the truth of change. Yet an acceptance and understanding of change is a deep spiritual insight that can transform our lives. Accepting change is at the heart of equanimity.

the eight worldly conditions

While change manifests in our lives in an infinite variety of ways, the Buddha said that there were eight basic ways in which we experience change. He called these the Eight Worldly Conditions. According to this teaching, change in our lives and how we tend to relate to it breaks down into four pairs of opposing conditions: pleasure and pain; gain and loss; fame and dishonor; and praise and blame.

Needless to say, we generally find the first half of the pair attractive, but would rather do without its partner. Yet, they come together, we cannot have one without the other.

Wouldn't life be great if we never lost anything? Good luck. We live in an ever-changing world where bad things happen as often as good. But this fact is not really the problem. The problem is that we *want* life to be good all the time. We want the desirable half of the pair never to change or pass. When we have the pleasurable side we are happy—ah, what a good life! But then we are shocked and disappointed when we receive life's inevitable pain. We get attached to what is pleasurable, and have aversion to what is unpleasurable. It sometimes works that the amount we are attached to something is the amount we suffer when we get the opposite.

Let's look at the pairs one at a time:

pleasure and pain

Life is, of course, a mixture of the pleasant and the unpleasant. And sometimes we have experiences that initially give us pleasure, but after a certain point make us unhappy, or vice versa.

the eight worldly conditions

Pleasure	*and*	Pain
Gain	*and*	Loss
Fame	*and*	Dishonor
Praise	*and*	Blame

Have you ever dated someone and assumed you would be happy with that person forever? Then a few months later you discover that you are annoyed by him or her. Pleasure shifted into displeasure. And it works the other way, too. Suppose the unpleasant task of cleaning your room one day feels satisfying. How strange!

gain and loss

Something gained in your life is not guaranteed to be there the next day, whether it be something found, given to you as a gift, or even earned. Anything that is "yours," from an article of clothing, a book, to someone's love could be lost or stolen or simply taken away. How many times have you lost a favorite earring? Has your bike ever been stolen? Have you ever lost a pet, your standing in school, or have a boyfriend or girlfriend tell you they just want to be friends? Maybe you lost a friend you counted on, or even your health. And even if you manage to hold on to most of what you possess, in reality, at some point you will die and leave it all behind.

fame and dishonor

You may have had a moment of fame in your life. Perhaps an article you wrote was published in the school paper, or maybe one was written by someone else about your accomplishments. But fame can switch to dishonor in a moment. What if someone spread rumors that the author or the subject of the piece was stuck up?

Sometimes I think about celebrities who were famous when I was younger. Where are they now? Once I saw a magazine article about what happened to child TV stars when they grew up. Many of them got addicted to drugs, some got arrested and sent to jail, others lost all their money. Most of them are no longer working actors, and you wouldn't know who they are today. While occasionally there is an uplifting story, fame is often fleeting, and even the most celebrated star may find him or herself on the cover of a tabloid. Even the Buddha himself was sometimes the object of ridicule.

Many of us derive our self-esteem from praise. When we don't receive it, we feel awful, like failures or unworthy human beings. Most of us hate to be criticized. The slightest comment by an older brother or sister can embarrass us. Wouldn't it be nice to hear only approving things about ourselves?

When I was in high school, I received a lot of attention from my teachers. Every time I got a good grade, I would feel like I had done something worthwhile. More importantly, it made me feel that I *was* worthwhile. With each "A", I felt recognized and valued.

The occasional bad grade would devastate me. How could this happen to me? How could *I*, who always excels, do poorly? I would get depressed and vow to work harder. I did not then understand the truth about the world—that it is always changing, and if I based my self-esteem on what my teachers thought of me, I was sure to feel bad, at least some of the time.

handling change

The Buddha's teaching shows us that it is not what we are faced with in life that is important, but how we handle it, our relationship to it, that matters. When difficulties happen, we tend to take them personally, either as an injustice or as if they were our fault. The Eight Worldly Conditions tell us that it is normal for our lives to be filled with change, both positive and negative. But it is useless expending our energy to try to sustain the pleasant and keep out the unpleasant. There is another way, the way of equanimity.

My friend Allison was dating Steven for six months. They were not especially compatible and soon things began to go wrong. When he broke up with her, she called all her friends *and* some of his friends, saying, "He's such a jerk, why did he do this to me? I never should have gotten involved with him. I'll never have a new boyfriend again. . . ." and on and on until her friends couldn't stand it any more.

Another friend, Manuela, also split up with her boyfriend, Kevin. She too felt sadness and a sense of loss, but she had an uncommon equanimity about it. She said:

I can't explain, but somehow inside me I knew that things don't last forever. I was incredibly sad, yet I didn't feel like things shouldn't be this way.

After her break up, Manuela took long walks in the woods and entered psychotherapy. She decided to use this time as a chance to learn about herself. Later she talked to me about the breakup with clarity and insight:

We were drifting apart and I didn't want to admit it to myself. I see now that I choose boyfriends who don't actually want to be in a relationship, and then I get mad at them for not being there.

Clearly these two young women both experienced a breakup, but had entirely different reactions to it. One was caught in her resistance to a change she found painful; the other was able to find equanimity within herself, and was thereby able not only to gracefully weather the change but also to learn about herself because of it.

We can't control events in our lives. There is always another mosquito. People we love unfortunately get sick. Relationships break up. We don't get into a college we want. Pets die. Frequently wonderful things happen as well. We meet a guy or girl who has all the qualities we have dreamed about, we score the winning goal, we discover a new activity we really enjoy and find we have a talent for it.

But all of these are worldly conditions that are subject to

w i d e   a w a k e   ·

change. If we hang tightly, trying to make the desirable things in life last forever, we will suffer. If, when things are undesirable, we resist them—"This shouldn't happen to me!", or blame ourselves, others, or the world, we will also suffer.

If instead we can develop equanimity and meet the changing conditions of the world with balance, calm, and even-mindedness, we will experience positive changes in our lives. We will suffer less because we will ride the changes of our lives rather than fight them. We will maintain an openheartedness, readiness, and sense of inquiry. Our minds won't be so uptight! We will feel lighter, happier. People will be more relaxed with us and might even enjoy our company more. We will be manifesting in our lives an acceptance and understanding of the Eight Worldly Conditions. Seventeen-year-old Alex described how being equanimous affects his life:

My friends respect me because they say I'm balanced. Whenever we lose a game or they break up with their girlfriend they always call me. Andrew said it's because he can count on me to be real. I'm right there for people encouraging them to face life in a real way. Sure, I get sad when bad things happen to kids, but I also know this is the way the world is. Best thing to do is try to be as at peace with it as I can.

apathy is not equanimity

The feeling of "I don't care, it doesn't bother me" is not equanimity, but indifference and disconnection. We can be confused by apathy and think it is equanimity, but in truth they are easy to distinguish. Apathy contains aversion rather than being balanced. Apathy does not acknowledge or accept, it simply refuses to deal with what is going on. It is expressed as rejection or denial. Fifteen-year-old José experienced apathy masquerading as equanimity after the death of his sister:

The summer before my sister was planning to go to art school, she got in a major car accident and died after being in a coma for weeks. We were really close, and when she was in the hospital I sort of went into shock—like automatic pilot. I thought, I can deal with this. I acted cool. People would ask me how I was doing and I'd just say, "Yeah I'm over it, gotta get on with your life." But inside I was burning up with pain that I couldn't face.

In truth, equanimity is not at all apathetic or passive. Nor is it getting so caught up in something that we lose our balance. For example, it is not equanimity to say, "Well yes, people are starving in Africa, but that's their fate. I mean, what can I do about it?" Nor is it equanimity to say, "My God! People are starving in Africa! I'll do everything I can even if it kills me!" Equanimity lies right in the middle. We experience concern and connection to our own or another's suffering. But we don't get so overwhelmed and caught in the suffering that we lose our clear-sightedness and focus. With equanimity we have great concern and love for the world, and we can work for change with an even-minded, realistic compassion.

The Vietnamese Zen master Thich Nhat Hanh tells a story of the boat people who secretly left Vietnam in the 1970s to escape political persecution. He said that often the seas were stormy and dangerous. Most of the people were terrified, as the boats were rickety, and they had a long way to go to get to safety in Malaysia or Hong Kong. People would be crying and panicking, and sometimes the boats would capsize. However, if there was just *one person* on the boat who was calm and maintained equanimity, the rest of the people would calm down. Then the whole boat would reach safety.

developing equanimity

One of the most effective ways to develop equanimity is through the practice of meditation. Meditation teaches us to be open and accepting of whatever arises in our experience. The next section of the book is devoted to learning the basics of meditation, what it is, how to do it, and how to work with difficulties. We can see for ourselves how equanimity is developed.

However, we can also develop equanimity in our lives at any time. Try to pay attention to situations in your life that seem either strongly positive or negative. Notice how seriously you take the situations, and how you react to them. Do you wish deep down that a pleasant experience will last forever? Or do you worry that an unpleasant experience will never go away? How much energy do you expend trying to keep life pleasant?

As you begin to understand how your mind works, see if you can be less reactive. When you are in a boring class at school, instead of getting angry or spacing out, remind yourself of the truth of change. When you disappoint your parents, and you get angry with yourself, remind yourself of the peace that comes from a balanced mind. Try to let go of judging yourself. When you lose your keys for the third time this year, remember the Eight Worldly Conditions, and don't be so harsh on yourself. The difficult things in your life will be much easier to bear with equanimity. And when wonderful things happen, please rejoice and enjoy yourself, but keep in the back of your mind that they too will change. This will help you when the inevitable shift happens. See if you can cultivate a mind that says, "I am willing to be present with whatever arises, no matter what it is."

In the end, equanimity cannot be forced. As we develop equanimity, we learn that we don't have to push away what is unpleasant and we don't have to run after what is pleasant. We don't have to build traps to get the "mosquitoes" out of our lives. Instead, we intuitively accept the truth of the Eight Worldly

Conditions. We create a flexible, strong, and capable mind that peacefully coexists with all life's mosquitoes. We learn we can inspire others, because we have the courage to be present with all of life.

exercise your changes

Review in your life when you have experienced the Eight Worldly Conditions:

* pleasure   * pain

* gain   * loss

* fame   * dishonor

* praise   * blame

Can you remember examples of when you had one of these and it quickly changed to the other? How did you feel? What did you do?

part two

learning to meditate

g e t t i n g   d o w n   t o   i t :
m e d i t a t i o n   i n s t r u c t i o n

> If you can't find the truth where you are, where do
> you think you will find it?
> —the Buddha

> Mindfulness is the miracle by which we master and
> restore ourselves. Consider, for example, a magician
> who cuts his body into many parts and places each
> in a different region—hands in the south, arms in the
> north, legs in the north, etc. And then by some
> miraculous power, lets forth a cry which reassem-
> bles whole every part of his body. Mindfulness is like
> that. It is the miracle which can call back in a flash
> our dispersed mind and restore it to wholeness so
> that we can live each minute of life.
> —Thich Nhat Hanh, *The Miracle of Being Awake*

We can discuss the many teachings of the Buddha, or
we can study aspects of Buddhism, but the only
way we will really understand the wisdom of the
Buddha is to put the teachings into practice. There is no better
way to have a practical, personal understanding of the principles
we have so far introduced than to embark upon a meditation
practice. Meditation is a cornerstone of Buddhism. It is the pro-

cess that makes the teachings come alive. This section of the book is the "how to" part. The section offers meditation instruction and directions on how to work with obstacles and difficulties that arise as you practice.

We can find meditation practices in religious and spiritual traditions all over the world. Meditation is about different ways to cultivate and explore our minds. These traditions offer four main kinds of meditation. First, in *reflection* meditations we sit quietly and reflect on a topic. We use our intellect to help us better understand a concept, situation, or something about ourselves. Prayer is another kind of reflection meditation. Second, with *cultivation* meditations, we deliberately try to invoke qualities or feelings such as compassion or lovingkindness. Third, in *concentration* practice, we focus on one object like a candle or word to bring our mind to a one-pointed strength. Finally, there is *mindfulness* meditation, sometimes called *vipassanā,* or insight meditation, which we will focus on in this book.

Mindfulness is a quality of mind that stays connected and aware of whatever is happening. It does not forget whatever it is aware of. In mindfulness meditation, as we calm our mind and develop moment-to-moment awareness of our breath, sensations, emotions, and thoughts, we gain insight into ourselves, our lives and the world.

Insight and knowledge are not the same thing, although they are easy to confuse. Books and teachers provide us with knowledge, facts, and information, which we accumulate and stuff in our brain. Knowledge is important. We wouldn't be able to function well in the world if we did not know how to read, find our way around, feed ourselves, or take care of our bodies.

However, insight is entirely different. It is our own inner wisdom. We might say that knowledge is in the head up, and insight is from the shoulders down. Insight is what we already know inside our hearts, but may not know we know! When we have an insight we feel familiarity, as if we have known it all along. Or we recognize its truth intuitively, rather than intellectually. We understand ourselves better, or learn a truth of the world, such as how quickly things change, and say, "Oh, of course! I can't believe I didn't see this before! It seems so obvious." Something inside clicks.

Meditation is a perfect tool for developing insight. The more we calm and quiet our minds and go inward without being distracted, the more insights will spontaneously arise. They may be insights into our emotions or habits like Don, a sixteen year old, noticed on a meditation course:

> I had been meditating for a number of years, attending a yearly 5-day teen retreat. Then on this one retreat, I had a breakthrough. That whole year I had been experiencing life as harsh and competitive. I was judgmental all the time of everyone else. I felt incredible pressure to perform, to be impressive. I knew I presented a really good façade. On this one retreat, after a few days of meditating, I had the experience of sinking beneath the façade, seeing how much I judge myself and how hard I have to work to keep it all together. I must not really like myself. Of course I felt a lot of pain and vulnerability when I saw this.

Or they may be insights into the dharma—the teachings of the Buddha as to how the world works. We may see the Four Noble Truths in our lives, or we may come to truly see impermanence in our body and mind. Most of all, we will learn to be equanimous with the changes in life that are happening inside us.

ten benefits of meditation

1. Encourages you to be more calm, relaxed, and less stressed out

2. Develops your concentration and sharpness of mind

3. Gives you insight into your body and mind

4. Helps you to understand truths about the world

5. Teaches you how to better handle difficulties in your life

6. Gives you an inner refuge, intuition, and guidance for making choices in your life

7. Increases your ability to be present, alive and to have equanimity in this changing world

8. Develops wisdom, kindness, and compassion

9. Increases your sense of humor

10. Helps you to wake up

the basics

location

Choose a place in your house or room where you won't be disturbed. It is nice if your meditation spot is not too messy. Some people like to set up a little table or altar with candles, incense, or photographs on it, but this is not necessary.

wide awake

equipment

Meditation is pretty "low-tech" and needs very little equipment. You can use a round, soft meditation cushion (called a zafu), but it is not necessary. Your bed or couch pillow work okay, too, if they are firm. Some people like to meditate sitting on chairs, which is perfectly fine. You also need a clock or watch so you can time yourself. You can set an alarm to go off to indicate you have finished.

time

Frequently people meditate in the morning after they wake up. Others meditate in the evening when they come home, or before they go to sleep. Choose the time of day when you are most likely to be alert and not too busy or distracted, or your siblings won't be bothering you. It is best to meditate at the same time each day.

Some people meditate for ten minutes when they start. Others feel they want to sit for a longer time. Many people find thirty minutes is a good and challenging amount of time for their daily practice. However, if you choose a length of time that is too difficult, you may give up right away. So pick a time that will be doable for you.

posture

Many people choose to sit on a cushion on the floor because they feel more stable. However, others feel that it is too painful to sit on the floor, so they prefer a chair. Either way is fine and it is good to experiment till you find the posture that works for you. The important thing is that you feel comfortable—but not too comfortable—so that you don't fall asleep. If you are in too much pain, you won't be able to meditate. So you need to find a compromise, a basically comfortable and stable position.

If you are sitting cross-legged on a cushion, for stability you want your hips to be higher than your knees. You want to feel stable at three spots: your two knees and butt. If your knees don't reach the floor, try sitting higher, or put other cushions under your knees. You want to be in a posture you can hold comfortably for the amount of time you have chosen. Try to keep your back upright, not frozen or rigid, but pretty straight. You may find that your legs fall asleep, but don't be alarmed, this happens to everybody. As your body gets used to the posture, your legs will fall asleep less frequently.

If you are sitting in a chair, don't slump, keep your back upright, but not stiff. If possible, try not to lean against the back of the chair, as you might fall asleep. Make sure both feet are firmly on the floor or use a cushion beneath your feet if your feet don't reach the ground.

In my tradition we meditate with our eyes closed. I recommend closing your eyes unless you are very sleepy or it feels claustrophobic. Your hands can rest on your knees or on your lap.

feeling the breath

"Feeling the breath" is a simple concentration and awareness practice that is the foundation of meditation. For now, read through these instructions just for understanding. Once you are ready to try meditating, it may be useful to have someone read this to you, or record it on a tape, so you will be able to put your full attention on your breathing.

Close your eyes and take a few minutes to simply notice what is happening in your body. What are the first few things you are aware of? How does your body feel? Is it heavy, light, uncomfortable, relaxed? Notice that you are sitting on the cushion or chair, nothing special.

Notice that you are breathing. Your body always breathes, but you rarely pay attention to it. There is no need to control your breath, just breathe normally through your nostrils (mouth closed). Bring your awareness to the place in the body where you notice breathing. For some people, the breath is obvious at the abdomen. You might notice your belly rising and falling, and feel all sorts of sensations such as pressure, motion, expansion, and deflation. Or you may notice breathing at the nostrils. At the tip of your nose you might feel sensations of coolness, or tingling, or tickling, or heat. Or, your attention may be called to your chest; the sensations you may notice there are similar to those in the abdomen.

Locate the place where you feel the breath most strongly. You may have to move your attention back and forth from your nose, chest, and abdomen until you determine which one is dominant. Once you choose, stick with it. Keep your attention on your breathing, focused on that spot, for the duration of the time you chose, being as mindful as possible.

Most people rarely pay attention to their breath. I am asking you not only to pay attention to something that may seem boring, but also to take interest in it. Use this practice as a *laboratory of discovery*: What can you learn about your breath? Is one breath similar to another? Try to feel each breath as it comes into being, exists, and disappears. What kind of subtle movements can you notice? Can you sustain your attention for more than one breath, or does your mind wander? Try to connect with each breath and sustain your awareness for the length of the breath, and then bring your attention to the next one.

distraction/thinking

Of course it won't be easy to keep your mind focused on your breathing. You will find yourself running off in thought and, in the entire ten minutes, you may only fully notice one single breath. That is quite normal. Usually when we try to focus on the breath we find ourselves floating away into past memories, future plans, fantasies, worries, and all sorts of stories. Your mind will continually be thinking, so please remember: *You are not trying to stop your mind from thinking.* Only in rare meditation states does thought stop. Thought is a normal part of our meditation practice. Later in the chapter we will discuss mindfulness of our thoughts.

For now, however, let's say you are trying to feel your breath and your mind wanders off for ten minutes into a great story about how you shot the winning basket three years ago. Simply be aware that you are thinking. That is it. The moment you notice you are lost in a story, you are no longer lost in a story. You are aware. If you let go of the story, you will be right back in the present moment easily.

Some people are helped by saying to themselves the word "thinking" to remind them that they have been lost in thought and not paying attention to the breath. "Thinking" is not said in a judgmental way, but in a calm and respectful way. It is a soft whisper in your mind. Then you go back to the breath.

Wandering off your breath may happen a hundred times in one sitting. It doesn't matter. Simply try your best to be aware of your breathing and when you wander off, notice you have wandered and then come back to the breathing once again.

beyond the breath: awareness of secondary objects

From now on let's think of our breathing as "the anchor" of our meditation practice The meditation anchor is like an anchor of a ship, it keeps the boat from being tossed around the ocean, subject to storms, turbulence, and capsizing. This is what the breath will do. You can always return to it and it will stabilize you. Breath is your primary object of awareness—what you put most of your attention on. Once you gain facility with breathing awareness, you can soon become aware of many other aspects of your experience.

Awareness is not limited to breath. Awareness is the part of our mind that knows. And there are lots of other things the mind can know. The other objects of awareness that I will mention are called "secondary objects"—things that we become mindful and aware of when they become more obvious than the breath.

Let's say you are feeling your breathing, when suddenly you feel an itch in your left armpit. Rather than immediately scratching it, or trying to force your mind to stay on your breathing, let the itchy feeling become the object of your awareness. Pay attention to the itch. Notice and feel how strong it is, how long it lasts, how large an area it covers. Arouse in yourself curiosity about your itch. At some point it probably will go away. When it does, return to sensing your breathing. If it doesn't go away, continue to feel and pay attention to the itch. It is that simple.

Here are some secondary objects that you can become aware of.

sounds

Sounds are everywhere, inside and outside our bodies, in the room or on the street. Many people incorrectly believe that complete silence is required to meditate. Mindfulness meditation does not require silence. It can help to practice in a quiet room, particularly when you are beginning to meditate. However, sounds make excellent objects of meditation.

When I was a nun in Burma, workers were building wood

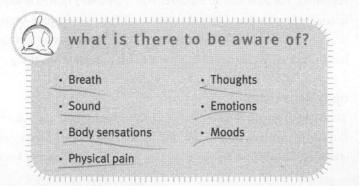

what is there to be aware of?

- Breath
- Sound
- Body sensations
- Physical pain
- Thoughts
- Emotions
- Moods

and concrete meditation huts all over the monastery while I was meditating. They hammered every day, even in one-hundred-degree heat! Every morning at nine o'clock the chain saws, drills, hammering, and shouting would start. At night, the workers put away the power tools, but played songs on guitar till midnight. At first I wanted to scream. I found the noise unbearable. I couldn't concentrate at all on my breathing. Later, though, I discovered that all I had to do was to notice the sounds, to make them an object of my attention, and they would stop being a disturbance. I began to listen to the various construction noises intermingling with one another, and to hear them as though they were a symphony.

Say you are feeling the sensations of your breath and a loud siren goes by your house—an ambulance, fire truck, or some other emergency vehicle. It is likely that you will be distracted by such a startling noise. Rather than forcing yourself to keep your attention on the breath, take the siren as your object of meditation. Bring your attention to the sound. Notice it in the same way you were noticing the breath. Can you hear the beginning, middle, and end of the siren? Can you notice its different vibrations? What is it like? Try to listen to it (and all sounds you encounter) as if it were a favorite piece of music.

As with the breath, avoid "making up stories"—thinking about and inventing reasons behind things—*"Hmm, I wonder what's happening, has there been an accident? Was it someone I know? Oh dear, it seems to be at the house down the street . . ."* Try to keep your attention on the sound itself, just as it is. When it changes or you no longer hear it, you can return your attention to your breathing.

body sensations
Throughout a typical day, a lot of body sensations go unnoticed. But the minute we sit down to meditate, they can take over our attention. In meditation some of you may be experiencing knee

or back pain. Others may feel chills or tickling or pricking sensations, or various itches. Our bodies experience a wide range of sensations from comfort to discomfort, to actual pain, and we can be mindful of all these sensations.

Feel your sensations just as you feel your breath: impartially, with interest and curiosity. When a body sensation becomes predominant (that is, more obvious than your breathing), focus on the sensation. Notice what you can about it—its location, its intensity. Don't "report" to yourself, "I'm presently experiencing knee pain and it's in my left knee and it's very distinct." Instead, use your powers of awareness to feel as much as you can of the sensation without making up stories. When it passes, or your mind grows tired of it, return your attention to the breathing.

physical pain

Sometimes in meditation, our sitting posture may first seem comfortable, but in a matter of minutes our body complains. If you experience pain, first try to get to know it just as you have been getting to know your breath. Feel what it is like. Notice sharpness, burning, motion, or whatever characteristics are there. Again, take the attitude of a scientist observing your experience.

As always, try to avoid making up stories: *"Oh my God, this may be serious! I might have ripped my cartilage. I may have to go to the emergency room and get a knee operation and then, I'll be in a wheelchair for six months and I'll never play football again."*

One fourteen-year-old meditator, Rajiv, who really got the hang of this, told me:

In meditation today I felt pain in my stomach. I didn't worry about it. I didn't make up a story about how I was sick or would have to go to the hospital. Instead, I paid attention to the small pain, which burned and grew. Then it shrunk and disappeared. I could notice my pain but it didn't bother me.

If you are paying close attention to the direct experience of your pain, you won't get carried away with stories. In Rajiv's case, the pain wasn't serious, but of course, you must not ignore pain if it is serious. You can tell the difference: If you get up from meditation and the pain goes away, you don't need to worry. If the pain stays, there is something you need to attend to.

If the pain you are experiencing is intense, try relaxing into it, using your breathing to soften it. Breathe deeply to calm yourself. If you find it difficult to stay focused on the pain, try moving your attention back to your breath for a while, returning your focus every now and then to your pain. If the pain becomes unbearable, don't continue to torture yourself, change your position to a more comfortable one.

The point of meditation is not to be a superhero. It is not to prove how well you can sit with intense pain. *The point of meditation is to cultivate an awareness that can be present with whatever is happening.* If your experience is so intense that you are not able to be aware of it, then you need to shift what you are doing so you can be mindful; this may mean moving your body to a more comfortable position. If you do decide to move, try to move slowly and see if you can be aware of the sensations of the body moving. In general, in meditation, we try to be mindful of pain without moving at first. If every time we feel pain, we immediately move to eliminate it, we will miss the opportunity to *understand* the pain. That said, there are a few important reminders for working with pain: First, know that pain is difficult to work with, both in meditation and life in general, so be gentle with yourself. Second, remember that pain is a fact of life—the First Noble Truth, in fact! There is nothing wrong with you because you are experiencing body pain; you are noticing the truth about the world, the way it actually is. We make a mistake when we are frightened of pain or think we are not supposed to experience pain. Pain is a fact of life. Third, remember that pain can cause your mind to tire, so don't devote all your time to trying

to be mindful of pain. You can always shift your awareness and
pay attention to your breath.

thoughts

Most of the day our minds jump around like monkeys. We are
constantly generating thoughts, hopping from one idea to the
next. This becomes all too obvious when we sit down to meditate and thoughts flood our mind. Believe it or not, however, we
can meditate with our thoughts rather than feel distracted by
them. This may surprise us, or seem contrary to what we assume about meditation.

Thoughts are simply words, sounds, voices, and images passing through our mind. Some thoughts are strong, such as "worries": *What if she wants to break up?* "Fears": *What if my mother gets
sick?* "Fantasies": *When I get out of high school I want to sail around
the whole world.*

What is the difference between "what if my mom gets sick?"
and "the sky is blue"? Both are thoughts. One thought has more
"charge" (or affects you more) than the other, but both are essentially sentences made up of words. The charge comes from past
memories, habits, associations, or our choice. Fears, worries,
strategies, and plans are all passing thoughts. So are judgments.

How many times a day have we thought *I'm so fat! That was so
stupid. This is so boring. He's way better looking than I am?* All day
long we make judgements about ourselves, others, and our experiences. But like fears and worries, judgments are just
thoughts. They may or may not be true.

When you notice an obvious thought, you can give it a mental label like "judging," "planning," "worrying," "blaming," "fantasizing," or (for general thoughts) "thinking." Notice what
happens to the thoughts as you label them, and then return to
your breathing.

You can experiment with your ability to notice thoughts.
Notice thoughts from time to time the way you notice sensa-

tions, sounds, or emotions. Then return your attention to the all-important breath. In general, it is difficult to pay attention to thoughts without getting lost in them, but it's certainly worth experimenting with.

emotions and moods

As you are meditating, emotions will come into your consciousness. They may be strong and obvious like an attack of anger, or they may be only a subtle blip on your radar screen. You can pay attention to them, as with sounds, body sensations, thoughts, and the breath.

When an emotion takes over your attention, see if you can be aware of that emotion. See if you can notice what it feels like in the body or where you notice it. Is it a burning sensation in your belly or a tightness in your throat? Is it weak or strong? Does it last a long time or quickly go away?

Also, you can notice any thoughts that accompany the emotion. Say you are feeling sad, you may be thinking you are a terrible person who never treats your sister well. This is a thought. In this particular example, a "judgment." Your mind could spend hours on the thought, wondering why you are feeling so unhappy. But just notice it.

Sometimes in meditation you also become aware of other mental states—moods or attitudes—passing through you like sleepiness, restlessness, boredom, or excitement. These seem to be more in the background than an emotion, which may seem central. If you find yourself experiencing any of these, try to keep awareness of it in the background. Try to limit the attention you give it to about 10 percent, while you give most of your attention to your breath or other object of awareness. Our moods and attitudes are like background noise that colors our experience. However, if a mood seems very strong, pay attention to it and see what happens as you observe it.

I will talk about working with strong emotions in a later

chapter but for now pay particular attention to moods. If you notice, for example, you are particularly hating your experience, pay attention to that that. Sometimes when we hate something, we make a bad experience worse.

big sky practice

My teachers call a certain kind of mindfulness practice Big Sky Practice. In Big Sky, you don't use the breath as the anchor. You have no anchor. You put all the objects together. It is an "everything" practice (like an "everything" bagel—poppy, sesame, onion, the works). It can feel a little scary, or confusing ("What do I pay attention to?"), but see what happens as you experiment with it.

Imagine that your mind is a vast blue sky. Now imagine that all the objects floating by, sounds, breath, sensations, thoughts, and emotions, are like clouds temporarily passing through your sky. Can you treat them like clouds? The sky doesn't get upset when a rain cloud passes in front of it. Nor does it get particularly happy when a rainbow appears. Can your mind be like that?

There is no right or wrong way to do this practice. All you

mindfulness meditation in a nutshell

Sitting comfortably, we keep our attention on the breath as our anchor or primary object. When secondary objects such as sounds, sensations, thoughts, and emotions take our attention away from the breath, we shift our awareness and pay attention to them. When a secondary object disappears or no longer keeps our attention, we return to the breath.

do is notice. Be aware of anything that is happening in the moment: sounds, breath, sensations, thoughts, emotions. There is no order. Notice what is happening in this moment, then the next, then the next. . . .

daily mindfulness

Once you develop the "muscle" of being aware—and it *is* like a muscle developed through exercise—don't assume awareness only applies to the meditation cushion or chair. The cushion is just a training ground for bringing awareness to other aspects of our lives. Anyone can be aware anywhere, at any time.

When we are mindful, we know we are doing something as we do it. We fully inhabit our life and our body. A good daily practice is to try to notice what your body is doing. When you are standing in line for lunch, check with your body. What do you feel? Are there aches and pains?

When you are cleaning your room you can really get into it. What does your body feel like as you lift and tidy things? How about your mind? You can also notice what you are feeling emotionally, or what you are thinking. Are you resentful, enjoying, happy, miserable? Are you thinking about your love life or about the room? With practice, you can be aware of all these things.

Coach Phil Jackson invited meditation teacher George Mumford to teach meditation to the Chicago Bulls and L.A. Lakers. Learning mindfulness made them better basketball players because they became more aware of their bodies. The Lakers won the NBA Championship in 2000 and 2001! (how much of the win was due to meditation?) If you are playing sports, you can notice the feel of the ball on your fingers, the movements of your feet, where the other players are and what they are doing.

walking meditation

People usually think walking on water or in thin air is
a miracle. But I think the real miracle is not to walk
either on water or in thin air, but to walk on earth.
—Thich Nhat Hanh

Walking meditation is another practice that you can do virtually anywhere at any time once you learn it. No one even has to know that you are meditating.

To learn the practice, simply pick an area about ten paces long to be your walking path. As you walk from one end to the other, notice any sensations you feel in your feet and legs. You might feel pressure, or tension, or lifting, or moving, and placing sensations. Don't *think* about your feet, but *feel* them as they move. In this meditation, your feet are your anchor, like your breath is in sitting meditation. When your mind wanders, return your attention to the sensations in your feet and legs.

Try this practice at different paces: fast, medium, slow, even slow-motion walking. Walking very slowly may allow you to notice a lot more. Continue walking back and forth, for the determined length of time. Walking meditation is not about going anywhere.

As you develop the skill, you can do walking meditation in the hallways at school or any time while walking. Mindful walking brings concentration, peacefulness, and awareness into your day. Instead of thinking about where you are going, you are with your body in the present moment.

developing a daily practice

Meditation is like practicing the piano. If you practice a little bit everyday, you will get better. If you are serious about learning to play piano, you don't practice some days and slack off other days. You still practice, even if you don't really feel like it. Of course this applies to any hobby or activity you devote time and energy to like karate, gymnastics, or a foreign language. The same is true for meditation. The only way you will begin to understand your body and mind is with consistent practice.

Make a commitment that for one week you will sit ten minutes (for example) every day. Or pick a different amount of time with which you feel comfortable. For that week do the simple breathing meditation described in this chapter. Even if you don't feel like it, or are too busy or too tired on a particular day, still try it. Don't only meditate when you feel like it, but do the practice no matter how you are feeling. If you are miserable, be aware of feeling miserable! Remember, it is practice; you are not expected to be perfect. That is why it is called practice!

At the end of the week, evaluate. How were your meditation sessions? Did you notice improvement over the week? Were you able to stay focused? Were you able to meditate even when you didn't want to be there? What was your life like when you meditated every day? Did you notice a difference? Did you relate to people any differently?

Meditating with others can be extremely helpful and supportive. Find out if other people meditate in your town and join what is called a "sitting group," a gathering for people to meditate together. Maybe your town or city has a local Buddhist center that holds daily meditations. You can even start a group in your school.

deepening your practice through retreat

Many people begin meditating on a daily basis and later realize that they would like to do more of it. They may appreciate the calm and peace in their mind or be curious as to what it is like to meditate for longer periods of time. This is where a retreat comes in.

Retreats can last for one day, or a weekend, or a week, or a month, or even a year! Typically retreats are mostly in silence, and meditators alternate sitting and walking meditation practice every forty-five minutes or so. Meditation teachers offer instruction, give dharma talks, and hold discussion groups. Often retreats are held in beautiful natural settings.

Retreat is an incredible opportunity to deepen your daily practice. One of my favorite things to do is attend a meditation retreat. It gives me an opportunity to get quiet, rest, and develop insight into my body and mind. I believe much of the wisdom I have learned for dealing with life has come through meditation practice, specifically when I have gone on retreat. For retreat center listings, including retreats specifically for teenagers, see the appendix of the book.

reflection meditation

Another kind of meditation practice that you may find very useful is reflection meditation. It is used to reflect on important questions in your life, or topics of interest. To do this practice, simply find a quiet place to sit where you won't be disturbed, or go for a walk by yourself. Let yourself get calm and quiet to the best of your abilities, maybe by starting with some breath or simple walking meditation. Then bring to mind your question or issue. Let it circulate in your mind. See what pops into your head. Free-associate as you wish, but if you start to get too far away from your initial topic, remind yourself gently about your question. You may discover answers or new insights you never imagined previously. You can also read any chapter in this book and then do reflection meditation with the chapter, asking yourself how the teachings apply to your life.

exercise: brushing your teeth

Pick one activity that you do everyday and practice doing it mindfully. Brushing your teeth works well, but you can pick any routine activity that you would like to investigate.

As you brush your teeth, see how much you can be mindful of. Can you be aware of your arm reaching for the brush? Squeezing the toothpaste out onto the brush? How about lifting it to your mouth, and then moving it back and forth over your teeth? What about the sound and sensation of the bristles rubbing against your teeth? While you are brushing, you can also be aware of what you are thinking or feeling. What do you notice? Boredom? Annoyance? Are you thinking about the brushing or something else?

Practice this exercise every day for a week. Then add other activities that you do alone. Try to bring as much awareness as possible to each activity.

seven

the cloudy sky: hindrances to meditation

The mind is something more radiant than anything else can be, but because counterfeits—passing defilements—come and obscure it, it loses its radiance, like the sun when obscured by clouds. Don't go thinking that the sun goes after the clouds. Instead, the clouds come drifting along and obscure the sun.

—Ajahn Mun, Thai Buddhist teacher

One fateful night, Prince Siddhartha, the Buddha-to-be, vowed he would not budge from his spot under the tree, no matter what happened. It was enlightenment or bust! He sat and sat, probing deeply into the mysteries of his mind, refusing to move until he was fully awakened. According to the legend, for eighteen hours he was tormented by Mara—the god of Darkness. Mara sent his armies to attack Siddhartha, trying to prevent him from reaching his ultimate goal. The prince sat unmoving while the following "armies of Mara" (which may simply have been the prince's internal demons) assaulted him:

[Mara,] your first squadron is sense-desires, your second is called boredom, then hunger and thirst compose the third. And craving is fourth in rank, the fifth is laziness, while cow-

ardice lines up as sixth, doubt is seventh, the eighth is malice. Gain, honor, and ill-won fame, self-praise and denigrating others, these are your squadron.

The Buddha must have had a torturous night! Yet, he was able to withstand these demons. All night he probed more and more deeply into his mind, and by dawn he had attained enlightenment.

Because the Buddha understood challenges so well from his own experience, when he became a teacher he was able to clearly explain for others the "hindrances" one encounters in meditation practice. A hindrance is something that obstructs us or gets in our way. If we are walking down a forest path with tangled vines that cause us to trip and fall, we are hindered. In Buddhist terms, hindrances are states of mind that give us trouble. When we are meditating, if sleepiness or boredom arise, we often feel we cannot meditate properly. Our meditation practice feels ruined. We have "tripped" on the hindrance along our spiritual path.

Experiencing these hindrances can be very painful and demoralizing. In our own meditation practice, we may find ourselves falling asleep in every session for a week. We may go through periods of doubt, wondering why we ever started this practice in the first place. We may be plagued by food cravings, sexual longings, and fantasies. We may feel angry, fearful, or judgmental. All of these are classical hindrances on our spiritual path.

Although hindrances can feel all-encompassing and defeating, the good news is that they are absolutely workable and are a natural part of everyone's spiritual journey. Over time we become more skilled at identifying and working with them. Hindrances will probably never fully disappear, but our attitude toward them may change. We will know how to deal with them and we won't see them as something wrong, or something that shouldn't be there. We can meditate *with* the hindrances.

In the last chapter we compared our minds to a big, open sky. When our minds are clear, focused, and undistracted, hindrances are like clouds, a natural part of the atmosphere, and a natural part of our minds. Some are heavy rain clouds that stay in the sky for days, and some are sweet and fluffy like cotton candy. Try not to judge your clouds or view them as a problem, or as something that does not belong in your Big Sky. We can learn to pay attention to the vast sky of our mind with all the "clouds" in it.

The Buddha told us that the main method for working with the hindrances is simply to become aware of them. If you are trying to meditate and experience any of these "clouds," try not to get upset and think that your meditation session is ruined. For example, you might think, "Oh, if only I weren't sleepy, then I could meditate." Instead, sleepiness becomes your meditation. You are not waiting for the sleepiness to stop so that you can finally meditate.

Just become aware of the hindrances, call them by name, and they may disappear. Even if one sticks around, we don't have to view this as a problem; it is simply what is happening in the moment. The five chief "clouds," or hindrances, that are commonly talked about in Buddhist meditation practice are wanting, aversion, sleepiness, restlessness, and doubt.

the five hindrances

1. Wanting

2. Aversion or hating

3. Sleepiness, sloth (slowness), and torpor (lethargy and dullness)

4. Restlessness and worry

5. Doubt

wanting

Wanting is a familiar cloud and the first of the five hindrances. When you have a pleasant experience, usually you want more of it, you want to prolong it. Or when you don't have something pleasurable, your mind remembers and wishes for it: "If only I had . . ." Wanting is the natural response of the human mind to pleasurable experiences or thoughts.

Any of you may experience the wanting mind when you have desirous memories or fantasies of a person, delicious food, a relationship, a fantastic experience, a material object. You don't even have to desire concrete "things," you might have visions of receiving recognition, attention, popularity, or even desire attaining a blissful state of meditation.

Wanting is not the memory or the object itself, but is the underlying feeling that fuels (increases and prolongs) the pleasant memory, desire, or a fantasy. Wanting is not the sexy guy or girl; they are *what* you want. The feeling of trying to have or possess the object is the wanting. When the wanting mental state arises, it is almost as if you are mentally leaning forward, not being centered, not in your body. You are looking towards the object to make you happy. One can actually feel the wanting energy—maybe centered in the gut or heart—towards the object.

At times there may be nothing specific you want. In that case, wanting can be very subtle—more like a slight feeling that what you are experiencing right now simply is not good enough, you want something else. The wanting mind desires this moment to be different, it does not find satisfaction with things as they are. It is a mind that cannot "just be."

Generally, when we are dissatisfied with the moment, we head off into the mental realm of memories or fantasies. Or, the slightest memory or vision of something desirable can enchant us. We can spend hours lost in fantasies or pleasant memories.

Ian who is eighteen, had a typical experience of the "wanting-mind" during meditation:

> *I had a great time meditating the other day. Well, I was supposed to be concentrating on my breathing, but the prom is coming up, so I spent the whole meditation designing what I would do the night of the prom. I imagined renting a limo, then I saw me and my girlfriend going out to a fancy dinner at this Italian restaurant she loves, then dancing at the prom, then I imagined how we would stay up and watch the sunrise. I saw the show in front of my eyes.*

Because the idea of the prom is so pleasant for Ian, his mind kept dwelling on it, inventing and imagining different scenarios. Wanting keeps our mind spinning in fantasies, memories, and stories.

Now this wanting may not feel like a hindrance. Your meditation period might seem to pass quickly because you are spinning out and prolonging a wonderful fantasy about a person, a material object, or memory. You might spend several enjoyable hours imagining your weekend plans, your dream boyfriend, or the lyrics to a song you want to write. "What's so bad about that?" you might be thinking. "How is it a hindrance? Meditation sure passes fast, and it's fun!"

Well, that is true. Fantasizing can be a lot of fun. The only problem is when you are caught in your fantasy or memory, you are not meditating. If you are lost in your desire, you are not in the present moment. You are not learning much about your body and mind. You are merely somewhere in a story about reality, not present in reality itself. Although stories are compelling at times, you get caught replaying them again and again. And life passes you by.

And truthfully, fantasizing is pleasant, but the actual feeling of desire is not pleasant. See if you can remember what it feels like to want something and not be able to have it. Have you ever had unrequited love—falling for someone who had no interest in you? This feeling hurts!

Luckily, you can work with this hindrance. You can use meditation as a laboratory to explore how often your mind chases future fantasies and past memories, and how frequently you want things to be different than they are. If you observe wanting in your meditation, you will get a direct experience and understanding of how attachment affects your body and mind. You will see for yourself the mechanics of the Second Noble Truth, suffering always has causes.

working with wanting

✳ If you become aware that you are lost in memory or fantasy, or are wanting something to be different (*if only I had more concentration*), try to experience the feeling in your body. What are the sensations? Where do you notice the craving in your body? What does wanting feel like? What are the thoughts that accompany it? If you can take interest in your desire, you may no longer take it so personally. You may realize that it is merely a thought and an energy passing through your mind that you have gotten hooked into. It is not a reality. Suddenly, the story stops being so interesting, the wanting feeling lessens, and you can return to your breath.

✳ It can be helpful to "name" your wanting; that is, simply say the word "wanting" in your mind. If you prick a balloon, it loses its air. When you are mindful of wanting, you "prick" the fantasy. *Mindfulness is the key to working with every hindrance.*

✳ If becoming aware of wanting doesn't work, try reflecting on your motivation for meditating. If you can remember your deeper reasons for meditating, for instance, to gain insights, to develop wisdom or compassion, then pursuing a desire may lose some of its attraction.

✳ You can also ask yourself: Is the object or objective that I am imagining going to provide me with lasting pleasure? Will the object ever change? Will I ever get sick of it?

✳ Finally, a fun way to work with recurring, obsessive thoughts (pizza, pizza, pizza) is to call them "tapes." Every time they pop into your head you can say "pizza tape" and notice how many times you say this. It could be hundreds! Noticing desires with humor can help our mind get out of its rut.

aversion

Aversion is the flip side to desire. It is a dissatisfaction with, or dislike of, anything—events, circumstances, or experiences in the moment: "Meditating is the most boring thing I have ever done in my life!", in the past—"I can't believe my teacher failed me!", or even in the future—"I know I have to babysit tonight and I hate it, why did I say I would . . . ?" Sometimes aversion is outright anger. Maybe you are furious at your sister for breaking your new CD player, and in meditation, all you can think about is how mad you are. Sometimes aversion is in the form of judgments of other people ("What is that person wearing?") or of yourself ("I'm so lazy!"). Other forms of aversion include grief and fear, as sixteen-year-old Susanna experienced:

> In meditation I kept thinking how I don't even want to walk around the halls of my school because I feel like such a geek. There's that gang of girls who is totally out to get me.

At other times, as with wanting, the aversion can be subtle, a mild sense of annoyance. Or, you have a vague feeling of *not* wanting the experience you are presently having. For instance, you may be experiencing knee pain (or a painful emotion, or a depressing memory, or . . .) and in truth, you wish the pain wasn't there. You want it to go away. You may even be disgusted or fearful of it. These are all forms of aversion to what you are directly experiencing in the moment. The overall feeling is that your current experience is not admissible.

Sometimes you have "layers" of aversion. You are distracted and annoyed with your knee pain, but then you are irritated with yourself for being annoyed by the knee pain. Or worse, you hate the fact that you hate the fact that you hate your knee pain!

Aversion is the antithesis of being connected, present, and awake in your life. Instead you are removed from your experience; you are mentally trying to push the unpleasant thing away or hold it at a distance. Often a self-righteous feeling accompanies aversion. You might feel that distancing yourself is what you *should* be doing. Self-righteousness might feel momentarily gratifying, but for the most part aversion is quite painful. I met fifteen-year-old Leo in a meditation class I was leading. He privately told me:

> It was my fifth time taking a teen meditation class, so of course I knew how to meditate and I just couldn't stand hearing the instructions again and again. It was so basic. As I meditated, I kept feeling better than everyone in the class, after all, they were all beginners. I felt pretty full of myself and that felt good. After a while I felt worse because all the other kids seemed to be having a good time and I felt distant and disconnected from them.

Aversion is a perfectly normal mental state; we all get annoyed, irritated, angry, and aversive at times in our lives. But if we can learn to be aware of the different forms of aversion in meditation, it can help us more fully to connect to the present moment. We will learn that we don't have to act on aversion, for instance, we don't have to quit meditating because our knee pain is unbearable. We don't have to get up from our cushion because we are so angry we want to punch someone. We can simply notice our anger. As we learn to be aware of aversion in our meditation practice, we gain an expertise in recognizing the forms of aversion and not taking them so seriously.

working with aversion

✻ As with wanting, your initial task is becoming aware of aversion, which means understanding the aversive feeling in your body and mind. Notice any physical sensations. Often you feel a burning sensation in your chest or belly. Sometimes just by noticing the disgust or annoyance you can pop the balloon. If you find it helpful, you can label it "hating" or "aversion."

✻ As you bring awareness to your feelings, you may discover layers of aversion. It is important to feel the top layer and then the ones below. "I am judging myself for being angry about this." "I am annoyed at myself for being fearful of this." If we try to be present with the anger or fear first, without becoming aware that we dislike these emotions, we will not be able to feel the underlying emotions fully. We will be pushing them away. Can you be present with all of these feelings?

✻ In Chapter 11, I will introduce you to an antidote to aversion called *metta*, lovingkindness. If, after experimenting with the above you find you are still having difficulty with aversion, you may want to skip ahead to that section before returning to this chapter.

sleepiness, sloth, and torpor

Everyone who meditates will experience the sleepiness cloud. Sometimes you meditate and fall asleep. Twenty minutes later the bell rings, and you wake up and think, *Hey, not a bad meditation session, I got a good rest!* At any meditation center you can see people sitting cross-legged on a cushion with their heads bobbing up and down as they snooze. They catch themselves, wake up, then fall right back to sleep. At a retreat center where meditators face the wall, my friend saw a man fall forward in sleepiness and bang his head. Everyone started laughing and that brought a lot of energy into the meditation hall. Nobody felt sleepy for the rest of the session, and the man wasn't hurt, just surprised.

Sleepiness can also come as sloth—laziness or slowness, and torpor—lethargy and dullness. A fourteen-year-old friend of mine refers to these as "sloth and torture." She says it feels disgusting, as if she were in peanut butter. One's body and mind feel thick, heavy, and too stuck in goo to meditate.

Sometimes the torpor and sleepiness is more pleasant than anything. Your mind feels dreamy and sweet, like you are in a sauna or the feeling you have right before you fall asleep. You will find it difficult to meditate when you experience this, as Janelle, who is fourteen, experienced:

> I hate sleepiness when I am trying to meditate. I just can't deal with it. I bet I'm fast asleep during most of my meditation, or in a dreamy sleepy world. I start off okay, but then after about ten minutes everything gets really foggy and feels awful. I keep trying to remember to be aware of my breath, but all I can do is fade in and out of consciousness.

working with sleepiness, sloth, and torpor

✳ Try to be realistic about your meditation. If you have been at school since seven A.M., baseball practice for four hours, done homework, and then you start to meditate at midnight, it would be no wonder if you are falling asleep! Try to do your meditation earlier in the day.

✳ If there is no apparent reason for the sleepiness, simply notice it. What are the body sensations? Where do you feel sleepy? Where is the glue in your body? If you have aversion to sleepiness, please notice the aversion, and then go back to the sleepiness. Can you label it as "sleepiness"?

✳ Sometimes we feel sleepy because we have painful feelings we don't want to experience. Sometimes falling asleep is an unconscious means of protection. Can you notice if anything else is going on that you don't want to feel?

✳ If sloth and torpor become unbearable and you can't be mindful of them, try these other strategies:

- Open your eyes, blink, and try meditating with your eyes open.

- Shift posture. Try standing up and continuing to meditate.

- Pull on your earlobes. (This unusual method is recommended in an early Buddhist sutta, or teaching).

- Try some fast-paced walking meditation.

✳ If all else fails, maybe you should take a nap.

restlessness and worry

When I first started meditating, my mind was like a Ping-Pong ball. I couldn't sit still for more than five minutes. I kept shifting my posture, moving my legs. First I felt itchy, then my knees hurt, then my back twitched. My mind was like a high speed movie chase. Sometimes I wanted to run screaming from my meditation cushion.

Restlessness is not always so extreme; it can even be more subtle than that. Sometimes you may feel that you can't focus on your breath or anything else. You may have cascading thoughts, one on top of the next. Sitting still may not be a problem physically, but mentally, you feel that you might as well give up.

Restlessness can also take the form of worry. Meditation is a great place to worry about anything: whether your girlfriend is going to break up with you, your parents are fighting, whether you will ever make a difference in the world, or even whether your red shirt goes with your new jeans. It can be endless and important. David, who is eighteen, asked me:

Why is it I'm always worrying when I meditate? I'm pretty sure I'm gay, and the second I sit down to meditate I worry about telling my parents and friends, and about how they'll react.

Everyone experiences the cloud of restlessness at some point or another when they meditate. For some people it is extremely common. For others, they tend more to veer towards the sleepy side of the pendulum. Still others experience both hindrances, never quite knowing what they will have to face in a given meditation session. Restlessness can be demoralizing because with all that mental and physical energy, meditating seems impossible. However, restlessness is a common cloud in our sky, and can be easily worked with.

working with restlessness and worry

✳ Begin by noticing your restlessness: "Oh, I'm restless." Where do you feel it in your body? Can you feel the underlying energy, anxiety, or speediness in your body? What kinds of thoughts are you having? Can you make your mind big enough to even be aware of restlessness? Can you label this combination of thoughts and sensations as "restlessness"?

✳ Please notice if you are judging or feeling aversion to being restless. These are common experiences. Restlessness and worry can feel *very* uncomfortable.

✳ If restlessness is so strong that you can't just notice it, you can:

- try to relax your body. You may want to move to a couch or chair. Generally when we sit upright, we expend some energy to keep our body straight and tight, which sometimes can make the restlessness worse, so relax your body by shifting your position.

- try paying attention to the sounds outside the room. Becoming mindful of sound might stop you from focusing so much on the restless energy of the body. You still will be mindful, but your mind will be more open and relaxed so the sitting will be more bearable.

✳ If you find that you are worrying a lot, try telling yourself, "Okay, if you want to worry, then you have five more minutes to worry." Let yourself worry for five minutes. Then stop, as you agreed. Or, make a different deal with yourself—you can worry all you want when the timer rings to end your sitting, but for now you meditate. By the end of the session, you may even forget to worry!

✳ If you have a particularly repetitive worry (What if Ani wants to break up with me? Will I ever get caught?), try naming it "worry tape," as you did in the case of recurring desire. See if you can catch it every time you worry about the same thing.

doubt

The fifth hindrance is doubt. You may have doubts about the meditation practice itself: *Am I doing this right? Is meditation a good thing? What does that woman who wrote the book know, anyway? Was there really even a Buddha, and did he teach this? Will it lead to anything? This is stupid. I don't feel any wiser or more insightful. Isn't learning to play the clarinet a better use of my time?* And so on.

Meditators doubt their teachers, the teachings, meditation; Everything can be doubted. The worst part of doubt is that you can't easily recognize when you are doubting because a doubt may be disguised as a belief, a revelation, or a discovery. You believe what your mind is telling you. Like seventeen-year-old Luis, who for a time, honestly believed he was wasting his time to meditate, because he didn't realize this belief was a doubt:

One day I was meditating and I began to think meditation was a complete waste of time. I believed this so much that I quit meditating. A few weeks later I realized I had been caught in doubt. Yeah, I started to meditate again.

Most painful is when you doubt yourself. You may think you are a failure at meditation or that you will never go far with the practice. Doubt can be demoralizing and cause lots of self-judgment, particularly if you get down on yourself for being a bad meditator.

Not only do our doubts concern our meditation practice, but each of us experience doubts about all aspects of our lives. During meditation, we can watch a variety of doubts arise about ourselves: *I shouldn't have said that. Does he even like me at all? I'll never learn anything in this school,* and others: *That teacher doesn't know what he's doing. My brother is never going to make it through high school.* Doubt can be extremely painful because we feel like we don't have ground to stand on—we don't know what is true in the world. We don't trust ourselves, our friends or family, and we can feel isolated and confused.

working with doubt

✳ Try to notice when you are in doubt: *Oh! There's a doubting voice in my head. Welcome doubt, you big pain. That's why I am feeling so bad because I was doubting my ability to meditate.* You can learn to label doubt as "doubt."

✳ Sometimes you are able to recognize doubt, but your doubts seem to you to be based in a truth you believe: "I know I'm doubting, but I *am* a rotten meditator." In this case, try to remember your motivation for practice and reflect on those benefits of meditation we discussed earlier in the book.

✳ If your doubt seems serious, why don't you try doubting your doubt? You are already doubting anyway, so take your doubt this one step further. Maybe you aren't the worst meditator in all of human history?

✳ As you practice, you will discover that doubt gets chipped away. The more you practice, the less you worry about whether or not you are doing it right. The more you see results, the more faith you have. Remember, we are not talking about blind faith, but confidence that comes from your own experience of practice.

clouds in your daily life

Not only do the five hindrances pop up to annoy you when you meditate, they make appearances constantly in your everyday life. During the course of one day you can feel wanting thirds at dinner, an aversion toward your boss, sleepy during late-night homework, restless when your friend is trying to tell you what he thinks is an interesting story, and doubting when you study for your driver's test. We probably encounter the five hindrances many times in one hour, but usually we don't recognize them; we simply assume that is how life is. However, as you become familiar with them in your practice, soon you will be able to recognize their presence in daily life. You may feel like jumping out of your seat during a class and suddenly you notice, "Hey, that's restlessness, I don't have to take it so seriously." When hindrances come up during your day, you can actually work with them just as you do in meditation, as sixteen-year-old Deena found:

> When I tried out for the school play, I practiced my monologue tons of times, thinking I would be great for the part. But at the audition I began to experience all these thoughts like "Oh, I'm a terrible actress, they'll never pick me." Suddenly after about half an hour I thought, wait a minute, this is doubt, *just like when I meditate*. So I said hello to doubt, and noticed that the thoughts were merely doubting voices and I didn't feel so nervous. I got into the play, although I didn't get the part I expected.

Remember, these hindrances are like clouds passing through, temporarily obscuring the radiant nature of your mind and the truth of who you are. They are great teachers for us, and are not a problem at all, merely difficulties that appear in our lives and change like the wind changes. Treat them with kindness and respect. Do not judge yourself for having them. Name them, "Oh there's a cumulus cloud!" "There's a storm cloud." And then, "Hey, no cloud on the horizon!"

exercise: working with hindrances

✳ In your meditation, pick one hindrance (wanting, aversion, sleepiness, restlessness, and doubt) to observe in your session, if it is obvious. Don't manufacture a hindrance if there is none. Notice how many times the hindrance comes into your mind in one meditation. You can even count it.

✳ The next day try another that is prevalent, and so on.

✳ After you have identified each hindrance, choose a hindrance you feel is the most difficult in your practice, and work with the practices I described in this chapter.

✳ Try to notice the hindrances when you are not meditating.

eight

turnaround time: working with strong emotions

If we can learn to be aware of feelings without grasping or aversion, then they can move through us like changing weather, and we can be free to feel them, and move on like the wind.

—Jack Kornfield, contemporary Buddhist teacher

During my teenage years, I had my share of emotional swings. For several weeks I would feel even-keeled, and then out of the blue, an incident would set me off on a nonstop crying jag. I would curl up with my mom on our comfy flowered couch, and cry and cry. Sometimes there was a good reason for crying, like my parent's divorce, or the end of a relationship. But often, the incident was minor: I just needed to cry. My mother sat there, listened attentively, and let me cry. I relied on her warmth and love to get me through the dramatic ups and downs of those times.

I remember one day at as I finished my sobbing, my mom put her arms around me and told me it was okay, that all this crying was good and healthy. "But Mom," I said, "I feel so vulnerable, I can't stop crying. Will I ever stop feeling so hurt?" That was when she told me this story: "Once there was a Zen master who was renowned for his wisdom and even-mindedness. Everyone placed high expectations on him, since he was the chief wise man of his country. One day his son died in a terrible accident. People rushed to his house to offer him solace, but also to see how a Zen master would react to such a great loss. They wondered, would his many years of practice enable him to remain strong, balanced, and peaceful in the face of tragedy? When they arrived at his home, the visitors found the master crying. They were shocked. 'How can you cry?' they asked, 'You are a Zen master! Zen masters are not attached!'

'Well,' he replied, 'Like you, I experience the pain of loss, so of course my son's death is causing me pain. However, the difference between you and me is that for me, the turnaround time is faster.' "

That story impressed me—deeply. At the time, I wondered if I could be like the Zen master: fully myself with all my emotions, yet able to "turnaround" swiftly. Could I learn not to be caught in the pain of my difficult emotions for such long periods of time? Could I learn to treat my emotions more lightly?

As the story of the Zen master illustrates, dharma practice is not about turning ourselves into unfeeling zombies. It is not about being passionless or emotionless. Having strong emotions is human. However, at times we can become tyrannized by our emotions, causing ourselves and others a lot of suffering. Because the Buddha knew that a balanced, peaceful mind leads to happiness, he offered practical advice to find happiness even in the midst of difficult emotions.

what *are* emotions?

Emotions are energies that pass through our minds and bodies. Emotions may feel like they are located in a particular part of the body, perhaps in our heart or gut—or they may seem to permeate every cell. Sometimes they visit briefly, sometimes they stick around. Emotions frequently have a physical component, like stomach pain when we are embarrassed or fearful, or tears or chest pains when we are sad. The physical feelings are usually accompanied by stories in our mind—recurring thoughts or memories. We can call this the "content of emotions." Content is all the things we think when we have an emotion: *This is the worst day of my life, I have never been so hurt by a person before, how could she have said that?* Also, we usually put some kind of label on our feeling: *Oh, I must be sad, I'm always sad* . . . But very often emotions come as one big clump of experiences, and we can barely distinguish the body sensations from the content, or from the label we give them.

In and of themselves, emotions are not a big deal, they are a natural part of life, but usually we don't experience them that way. Fifteen-year-old Olivia described to me the essence of the past two years of her life:

> *I am always upset about something. I am usually crying over my boyfriend, angry at my dad, disappointed about school, pissed off at society. Or then I get these bliss moments, like when things are going well with my boyfriend. I'm so happy I think I'll never come down. But then I crash and get depressed again. I never get a rest from my emotions.*

Remember earlier when we talked about dukkha? Well strong unpleasant emotions are dukkha, or suffering. The teenage years are awash in emotional suffering—from raging hormones to dealing with the pressures of school, friendships, dating, parents, work, and balancing first-time freedoms with new levels of responsibility.

reactions to an emotion

The main difficulty with an emotion is that we can rarely "just *be*" with it. That is, we can hardly stand to experience it exactly

as it is occurring in the moment, without having reactions to it
one way or the other. The emotion itself is merely a set of experiences—sensations, thoughts, associations, and labels, as I
described above. Some kinds of emotions are painful in themselves. Sadness hurts, fear is clammy, unpleasant, and disorient-
ing. June, a fourteen-year-old from the teen meditation class,
saw the painfulness of anger:

> I am constantly fighting with my mom. In the last year I have
> had more screaming fights with her than my whole life up to
> this point. I hate it and notice that I'm sick with anger half the
> time. Really, I feel nauseous, but she pisses me off and I
> can't help myself.

An emotion itself can cause us pain, but our reactions compound
our suffering. Our reaction is how we *relate* to the emotion.

One typical reaction many of us have to a painful emotion is
to want to avoid feeling it. We try to push it away because it
makes us so uncomfortable. This aversion is a hindrance from
the last chapter. Sometimes we numb ourselves, or cover up
feeling bad with incessant activity or too much TV, computer,
eating, sleeping, or drugs or alcohol. Avoiding an emotion often
makes the emotional pain worse. If we numb out or push it
away, the emotion may sit there inside us, festering, and then escape from us at an inopportune moment. Seventeen-year-old
Ray experienced something like this:

> When my parents got divorced, for several years I just
> couldn't deal. I didn't feel sad, I didn't feel much of anything.
> But the truth was that all the sadness was still in me. And one
> day, when my girlfriend and I were talking about breaking up,
> I turned into a maniac. It was like all the sadness and rage I
> had stuffed down in me flew out of my body and went
> straight for my girlfriend.

One night I was home alone, washing my dishes and had a thought to check my email. I went on line, found no new email, so I perused a few web sites, but that got boring, so I walked over to my bedroom, then down to my basement, then back up to my bedroom, lifted up a book, flipped through a few pages, got sick of that, turned on the TV, although I don't even receive any stations, called a friend, she wasn't home. Finally I collapsed on my bed. As I lay there, a feeling of worry came over me. I sensed a tightening around the area of my throat. As I paid attention to it, the contraction got more intense. Suddenly tears came. I realized I was scared and anxious about an upcoming project at work. I didn't want to face the fear, so the restless, busy activity had been a way to avoid the difficult feelings. As I lay on my bed, noticing the fearful feelings, I thought, *Well, it's only fear, I can face fear.* As I paid attention to it, the fear softened. In its place was courage.

Another typical reaction is that we may imagine or believe that a given emotion will last forever. We think and worry: *I'm sad now, I'm never going to be happy again in my life. I'm the saddest person I know. . . .* This makes the emotion into a larger problem than it originally was. We can feel overwhelmed by a small feeling, thinking it will be with us always.

We also might react to the emotion by judging ourselves for even having certain kinds of emotions. We may have been taught that specific emotions, like anger or sadness, are not allowed. Strong emotions are normally tricky to just be with, but when we judge ourselves for having the emotion in the first place, we give ourselves a double dose of negativity. When I was younger and I experienced strong sadness, I used to think that something was wrong with me. I would blame myself for having the sadness: "You're not supposed to get sad. You are supposed to be happy all the time, something must be wrong with you." And I would feel worse.

Is there any hope for this situation? Is it possible to work with emotions in a healthy way? Is it possible to take them more lightly? Is it possible not to act harmfully?

Of course. Remember the third of the Four Noble Truths; the Buddha said an end to dukkha (suffering) was possible.

working with emotions

Most people tend to either *repress* emotions (pretend that we don't have them or push them down somewhere into our bodies) or *express* emotions (go ballistic, threaten people, or hurt someone because we are angry). Neither of these are healthy ways to deal with emotions.

Instead, the Buddha offered us an alternative. He told us to be aware of emotions (or mental states) as they are happening. Essentially, this teaching is encouragement to "just be" with emotions. The Buddha said: *"When a mind of greed arises, a practitioner knows this is a mind of greed. When a mind of hatred arises, a practitioner knows this is a mind of hatred."* And so on, with any emotion, such as anger, fear, joy, and worry. In doing so, he said, *"We can see mental states as just our minds, not ours, not belonging to us."*

The Buddha was talking about a process known as "dis-identification." Dis-identification can lead to freedom from emotional suffering. Generally, painful emotions feel like a big deal because we are identified or *caught* in them; we believe strongly in them.

However, as we meditate we will see that even though emotions *feel* like a big deal, they are something that passes through us, like breath or sound, or body sensations. They change. They are not facts. They are happening in our body, but as the Buddha said, they "don't belong to us." From a distance, even a few days later, don't you sometimes think, whatever was it that made me so angry? This realization is also called "not identifying" or "dis-identifying"—not believing so strongly that an emotion is "mine," not taking an emotion so personally.

Dis-identification is dependent upon acceptance—allowing ourselves to fully feel the emotion and knowing that this emotion is acceptable. The thought "Oh no, I shouldn't be feeling this" is unhelpful. Or, "I am a bad person because I am angry/sad/fearful" is self-judgment. Well, in Buddhist terms, no emotion, whether pleasant or unpleasant is inherently wrong. Acting on an emotion may have harmful consequences, but the emotions themselves are not the problem. Emotions are a *very* important part of what makes us human. They add richness to life. That is why fully feeling an emotion when it comes through us is so important.

Dis-identification also depends upon investigation. If we can take interest in our emotions, examining them as if we were aliens from another planet, even, we won't be caught in them so completely. When we investigate emotions, we observe the components that make up emotions, which I spoke about earlier. We notice how they feel in our bodies, the stories we are telling ourselves about them, the labels we give them, and the reactions we are having to them.

Be an Alien

Imagine that you are an alien from another planet. You have the power to go inside a human's mind. So you go inside yours. As an alien, you wouldn't take personally any emotion you were observing. You would notice all the different sensations, thoughts, and feelings that make up an emotion. To you, these human emotions would be merely fascinating. Wow, humans are really weird! You might observe that "this human" is angry at his brother, or depressed about his relationship, or excited about starting his job. Aliens observe with a high level of curiosity and dis-identification.

steps for working with emotions: RAIN

One of my teachers, the vipassanā teacher Michele McDonald-Smith, taught a step-by-step process to relate to emotions when we are meditating. She uses an acronym, "RAIN": Recognize, Accept, Investigate, Not Identify:

1. Recognize

Michele invites us first to recognize the emotion while it is happening in our meditation. It takes some practice, but can be done. We can recognize sadness when it is occurring. We can know that we are happy, excited, angry, peaceful, or bored. When I am meditating I find it helpful to use a word in my head telling me what the emotion is: "sadness," "fear," "embarrassment," and so on. One word can help make a clump of emotions feel less overwhelming.

2. Accept

Acceptance is needed to "just be" with the emotion. We have recognized and named the emotion, but we need to find the courage to accept it. Rather than judging ourselves or thinking something is wrong with us for having the emotion, we simply welcome it, "ah yes, there's sadness." When you notice an emotion, see if you can remind yourself that this emotion is the truth of the moment, and there is nothing wrong with it. See if you can fully feel and be with the emotion exactly as it presents itself to you.

3. Investigate

Once you have recognized and accepted the emotion, you can learn to investigate it with curiosity and interest. What do you feel in your body? Do you feel a knotting pain in your stomach, for instance? Or does your heart hurt? What kind of stories are you telling yourself about the way you are feeling? See if you can observe a general feeling that can be labeled such as, *I sure am sad.* What kind of reactions you are having to the emotion? If you are angry, are you ashamed and wishing your weren't feeling angry?

4. *Not identify*

This step may happen automatically after we have gone through the other steps. Once we have recognized the emotions, accepted their presence, and then investigated what it feels like in the body, and the content of it, we will find ourselves taking the emotion less personally. We see that emotions really are a set of energies, sensations, thoughts, and labels. We may find ourselves less caught in them, we have dis-identified.

Please keep in mind a few important reminders. First, although this sequence is written linearly as a set of steps, often we go back and forth between the steps or find ourselves working on some of the steps simultaneously. This is fine. The steps are guidelines, and can be followed in a way that works for you.

Second, if it is not bearable to be with your anger, sadness, or anxiety, try to return your attention to a neutral or pleasant object such as your breath or a sound. Check in with yourself to notice how much energy you have. If your energy level is low, being mindful of your emotions will be more difficult.

Third, at times when we notice emotions and dis-identify with them, they actually disappear, what a lovely relief! But keep in mind, we are not trying to get rid of them. We are trying to see them clearly. Through clear-seeing, we take them less personally and we can act wisely. We can experience them, understand them, and then quickly turn around.

Finally, remember that emotions are difficult to work with. Some can be painful and you can be easily caught in them. Go slowly and gently as you work with emotions, and remember practicing with emotions is a lifelong task.

If you have had difficult experiences in your life (abuse, death of a family member, divorced parents), these memories or anxieties may arise when you are meditating. Sometimes these memories or other experiences in meditation are too strong or painful to work with on your own. Please seek support from a therapist, meditation teacher, or school counselor who is trained to work with difficult emotions, memories, and experiences. If you have suicidal feelings or thoughts about hurting yourself, it is very important that you seek counseling.

working with the steps

Arisha started a relationship about six months before she attended a ten-day meditation retreat. She had really been looking forward to the retreat, but when she sat down on her meditation cushion in the meditation hall, she found that all she could think about was her boyfriend. She couldn't keep her mind on her breathing. She became anxious and worried for the fate of the relationship and whether he was actually still in love with her. She wondered if they would still be together when she came home.

rain: steps for working with emotions

1. RECOGNIZE emotional states

2. ACCEPT that all emotions are a natural part of being human; this emotion is fine

3. INVESTIGATE and take interest in your full emotional experience

4. NONIDENTIFICATION—learn to take your emotions less personally. Be an alien!

She felt overwhelmed, but rather than obsessing, she decided to try to meditate with her feelings about her boyfriend. First, she *recognized* what she was feeling—sadness, fear, worry. Next she reminded herself that emotions were okay, even though she didn't particularly like the ones she was currently experiencing. So she let herself *accept* and be present with all the feelings. As she *investigated* the emotion more closely, she noticed the pain in her belly, the sense of loss. She noticed her mind telling her she was hopeless, she noticed how much worrying she was doing. She worked with these feelings whenever they came up over the course of her meditation retreat.

The feelings kept up for a few days. Then one day, Arisha was in the shower and she felt lonely. Suddenly she thought, "Wait a minute, I'm experiencing loneliness. It's just a feeling. It's not me." She felt relief wash over her. She began to laugh uncontrollably. She could be fully present with loneliness, but not take it so personally. She had *dis-identified*. Afterwards her anxieties and fears didn't go away, but they seemed to lessen. And she found she could recognize the feelings more quickly each time they entered her mind. She didn't take them so seriously.

Over time and practice, working with emotions in our meditation practice will be directly applicable to our everyday lives. Miguel, who we met earlier, ended up locked up for theft when he was fifteen, and learned meditation at seventeen through a program held at his juvenile hall. Now at twenty-one he is teaching meditation to other kids in juvenile hall. I asked him how his relationship to anger has changed.

> *A few weeks ago, I was teaching a yoga class in a juvenile hall and when my eyes were closed, one teen threw some tape he had pulled off the floor at my face. Because I was so*

concentrated I could tell it was him, and of course I got mad, I wanted to take the bell and bust him in the face with it. But I knew I didn't have to do that. Instead I noticed how angry I was, and decided to teach the kid something. I talked to him after class in a calm way, I said, 'If someone did that to you, what would you have done?' 'I woulda punched him,' he said. I said, 'I woulda punched him, too, but it takes a stronger person not to punch back.' When I said that, the kid saw how he brings stress upon himself.

After practicing meditation, it's ten times harder to get me in a fight. I used to fight rather than argue. I hated arguments. I'd rather fight. Now I ask myself is there anything worth attacking someone for? Now I know that the person is fighting me because they're needing to vent their emotions. I'm lesser than them if I attack them.

Like Miguel, we may find that over time and with practice, we will have more awareness; we will identify less with our transient states of mind. We will be able to act skillfully with emotions when they come up in our daily lives and can influence others in beneficial ways. We won't stop having our painful emotions, but our turnaround time may increase.

exercise your emotions

✳ Observe yourself closely for a week or two to learn your usual way of working with emotions. Do you tend to act them out or repress them? How did your family or your upbringing treat emotions?

✳ Next time a strong emotion comes up when you are meditating, go through the steps I have previously outlined in the sidebar for RAIN. What is your experience?

✳ Next time an emotion comes up when you are not meditating, see if you can go through the RAIN steps. Practice the RAIN steps with both serious and not-so-serious emotions.

✳ Pretend for one meditation session that you are an alien from another planet inside the head of a human (you). Write your observations.

part three

surfacing our inner goodness

nine

from self-judgment . . .

> A sage does not speak in terms of being equal,
> lower, or higher. Calmed and without selfishness, he
> neither grasps nor rejects.
>
> —Sutta Nipata 954

We are now entering the section of the book that is intended to help us explore our self-image. We will take the principles we worked with in the first section of the book, and the tools and practices of the second section, and apply them directly to the critical issues of self-esteem, self-hatred, and self-acceptance. We will use Buddhist wisdom to consider the possibility of freedom from this habitual and painful way of being.

> *"My boss is out to get me." "I'm too serious." "I'll never make it through school." "I'm different than the other kids, and everyone knows it."*

These are some of the voices we hear inside our heads all the time. They arise at the most inappropriate times, as if deliberately trying to make us screw up—just when we most need confidence. Sometimes rather than a single word of criticism, we hear a running commentary, like demons in our mind, reminding us how utterly inept we are. It can feel like we judge ourselves non-stop, all day long, on automatic pilot. Fourteen year old Sanjay expressed:

> *Whenever I don't do well on a test, the next voice I automatically hear in my head is, you're so stupid!*

No one likes to be criticized. Think about how we feel when someone judges something we did. We feel hurt. But often we are far meaner to *ourselves* than our worst enemies may ever be. If anyone ever said to us the kinds of things we say to ourselves, we would be shocked and insulted. How dare they? Yet we regularly say nonstop, judgmental criticisms, barbs, and insults to ourselves *inside* our heads.

judgment versus discernment

Saying "I am the ugliest person in school because my teeth are crooked" is different than saying, "My teeth are crooked." The first is what anyone would recognize as a judgment, while the second is a discernment.

Usually, a discernment implies a judgment of some sort, but in Buddhist terms we like to distinguish a discernment from a judgment. Discernment is a natural process occurring in the mind that perceives and recognizes the world. When we see a form in a certain four-legged, furry shape, we might discern that it is a dog, for instance. Our ability to discern tells us the shirt is clean, my hair is auburn, that flying metal object is an airplane in the sky. We are discerning all the time. In fact, we have to. We need to be able to discern all sorts of things from how hot a flame is so we don't burn ourselves, to who is worthy of our trust.

A judgment, as differentiated from a discernment, is something that has a value associated with it. Rather than merely seeing something as it is and recognizing it, we attach a positive or negative value to the thing we have discerned. Another way to see this is that unconsciously a "charge," or (usually) unpleasant feeling, is associated with a judgment, while the discernment is neutral. Usually when we judge ourselves we have an unpleasant feeling—judging is painful.

So an example would be, if we get on a scale and look at our weight, we can discern that we weigh 120 pounds. If we then think "One hundred and twenty pounds! I can't believe how fat I've gotten!", then we are making a judgment. See if you can notice the difference between discerning something about yourself and judging yourself for what you have perceived.

the origins of self-judgment

Since we now have a clearer understanding of what an actual judgment is, we might ask where they come from. We were not born thinking we were unworthy. A little baby does not compare itself to another baby and think, "She's cuter than I am." However, when children reach two or three years of age, they start to reflect the outside messages they have been absorbing.

Usually our parents or others who raised us, consciously or unconsciously, transmit messages to us about how we are supposed to be. The truth is, many parents—not all, of course—don't feel good about themselves either. Cycles started generations ago when children received judgmental messages from their parents, and these were transmitted to their own children, and so on. In a perfect world, parents would be supportive and loving and would only offer constructive, helpful criticism. But most parents aren't perfect. Some say that parents tend to see their children as extensions of themselves, so when parents don't feel loving toward themselves, they likely won't be loving toward their children. Maybe, since you were little, your parents sent you messages that you were too hyper, too serious, or too fat, as was experienced by fourteen-year-old Meena:

My mom was always saying to me, why don't you lose weight? She said she was a fat, unhappy kid and didn't want me to be like her. But she doesn't understand how much it hurts me to hear her say that. One day I wrote her a song and it was all about accepting me as I am and stopping criticizing and she still didn't get it. A few weeks later when I asked her to stop telling me I was fat she said, "What are you going to do? Write another song for me?"

Meanwhile, we are not only receiving messages that target us personally, but also broader, invasive cultural messages. The cultural climate in the United States is extremely competitive and superficial. Nonstop TV, movies, advertising, and popular magazines bombard us with messages of how we are supposed to look and behave, even what color our skin should be. Girls must be beautiful, thin, sexy, accommodating . . . and boys must be strong, masculine, unemotional, successful. . . . The American media even spreads a dominant cultural message to the rest of the world. Advertisements, film, and television tell people from different countries and ethnic backgrounds that to be happy they must look like beautiful, rich, white Americans. This is very disturbing.

And of course 99 percent of us do not meet those ideals. Few of us look like movie stars. Much of the world is not permanently happy, thin, white, rich, or successful. But since these fairly exclusive ideals shape our reality, when we don't fit them (and as noted, most of us don't), we can feel terrible about ourselves. Then we spend a lot of our time and energy trying to live up to these images, or feeling bad about not being them. Few escape from this awful, vicious cycle.

Nineteen-year-old Gin experienced the pressure of not fitting into cultural norms:

I'm Asian-American, which means I look nothing like you're supposed to look like in California. I'm not white, I don't have a lot of muscles, I'm not tall. But I'm also not some computer geek with pencils in his pocket like the stereotype of Asian people. At times I start to hate what I look like because nothing around me is reflecting back my image.

self-hatred

Self-hatred is truly an epidemic in the developed world. U.S. citizens have so much wealth, but they have a poverty of spirit. There is a very revealing story about His Holiness the Dalai Lama, the spiritual leader of Tibet, who was meeting with a group of Buddhist teachers from the United States and Europe. One of the teachers said to him, "A great obstacle to meditation practice of many of my students is extreme self-hatred. What can I do about this?" Apparently the Dalai Lama did not understand what the teacher was asking. He had to have the question translated from English to Tibetan about three or four times. Finally he asked, "Why would anyone want to hate themselves?" The Dalai Lama, from his cultural background of Tibet—high in the mountains in Asia—simply could not understand or relate to the concept of self-hatred.

While most of us are affected by self-hatred, we are not all affected equally, and some, very minimally. Some people may feel more supported by family or friends and are better equipped to deal with feelings of unworthiness. Some of us may not experience self-hatred at all. We may feel that we are an okay person, that we have our flaws, but that they are not overwhelming and are workable. If this is the case, you may choose to skip the rest of this chapter.

However, many of us, especially in the developed world (and it is unfortunately infecting the rest of the planet) are tormented by these voices of self-hatred. Every person has had to find his or her own coping mechanisms to deal with the voices and negative self image. Some become depressed, others angry, antisocial, or violent (witness Columbine and other such events). Some may rebel against ridiculously impossible "norms." Some may go numb, become apathetic, or disillusioned. For others, the hating feelings are so intense they might contemplate or attempt suicide. Others cut themselves because they are so numbed out, as was the case for Delia:

> *When I was in tenth grade I started cutting myself. I would take this razor and stand in the shower and slide it over my arms. I'd watch the blood flow down the drain and think about how meaningless my life was. It was the only way I could feel something at all in my life—the pain and the dripping blood.*

Through practice, we will see that these self-judging voices are real and painful, but also something that does not have to take control of our lives, and does not have to lead to destructive, alienating, or hurtful behaviors. Buddhist practice can help with this difficult area in our lives.

measuring ourselves

In Pali, the language of the Buddhist scriptures, there is a word *mana*, (mah-na) which means "measuring," "pride," or "ego." Another translation is "comparing." Mana comes in three different forms: better than, worse or lesser than (when applied to ourselves, we usually recognize this one as self-hatred or low self-esteem), or equal to. Our minds are continually comparing or measuring ourselves up to others or to our past experiences. At times we may think very highly of ourselves, "I'm great, wonderful, the best student." At other times, "I'm the worst, I'm no good, I'll probably fail out of school." And at still other times, "I'm just average, the same as everyone else." Of course some comparing is not judgmental. "My hair is shorter than her hair" is merely an observation (or discernment, as we talked about earlier) in regard to mana, the Buddha was talking about comparing that puts one person above or below another.

The Buddha described mana 2,500 years ago, so to some degree, comparing is normal, even universal. Even thousands of years ago in ancient India people were judging themselves and comparing themselves to others. It did not matter if they were villagers, soldiers, or kings. The Buddha recognized that our minds have been conditioned to compare. It is only a fully enlightened being who does not compare him or herself to others.

However, the Buddha pointed out that anytime we compare ourselves to others, we are creating a fixed sense of self—that is, we are locking ourselves into beliefs about who we are. The Buddha recognized that we humans are obsessed with our "self" or "ego." When we compare ourselves to others, we have a strong sense of "me" or "my" that is either superior or inferior, and so comparing strengthens our sense of self or ego. Even when we are feeling equal, there is still a sense of *me* arising. Although comparing is normal, but the problem is that we are not seeing the truth of who we really are.

The truth is that no single quality of our identity is ever static. In Buddhist terms we call this *anatta* (ah-na-ta) that there is no permanent, fixed self that we can point to. We are a set of qualities, characteristics, identities, and beliefs; we may take on or drop labels and roles, which are all constantly changing. You may consider yourself to be lazy, motivated, a hockey player, or, the hottest guy or girl in the school, the best dresser, or the most unlikely to succeed, but you are never continuously or permanently any of these things, as seventeen-year-old Natalie saw:

In ninth grade I cut my hair short and dyed it neon blue. I wore lots of black that year, and everyone saw me as cool and removed, kind of a punker. Over the summer I hung out with a different group and when I went back to school for my sophomore year, my hair had grown out and the color had faded. I was into studying more, which no one expected, least of all me! Kids didn't know how to relate to who I was anymore. They kept expecting me to be the same as in ninth grade, but I was different and didn't want to be pigeon-holed.

If we look closely at our life we will see that we may put a judgment or label on ourselves at one point, but the label may not hold up; it may be no longer true in a week, a month, or a year. Yet, we tend to want to cement our identity around these labels or comparisons. Understanding anatta means we don't get locked into an identity as we see it is not us. In Buddhist teachings we don't have a fixed, unchanging self. It means we don't take identities, labels, comparisons or judgements so personally. They are not us. They are impermanent. Not taking things too personally is one way of thinking about the term anatta.

working with self-judgments

We can use Buddhist practice to work with these self-judgments, to keep ourselves from being locked into a sense of "this is who I am, I am stuck with it." Mindfulness practice is extremely helpful for learning first to *recognize* self-judgments, to *accept* them, *investigate* them, and *not to identify* with them—the four RAIN steps we worked with in the previous chapter on emotions. If you need to, refer back to these steps, as they are a useful tool for working with self-judgments. The following exercises will give you additional tools to help you get a handle on self-judgment. Our goal is to develop an ability to take our judging voices more lightly. We can learn to see them as voices that float through our minds, not personal, and not as permanent, unchanging reality.

becoming aware of judgments

One of the most helpful skills you can learn is to become aware of making judgments, particularly those that are directed at yourself. Meditation is a fantastic laboratory for exploring the phenomenon of self-judgment. The moment you sit down, an army of judgments jumps into your head and attacks you: "This sucks, meditation is boring, I'm a lousy meditator, I hate my supervisor at work, my thighs are too fat, this is stupid, why did I ever start . . ."

Meditation provides the chance for you to observe your mind and learn how it works. You get to see just how incredibly judgmental you are. However, rather than judging yourself ("I'm so judgmental") you merely notice what is happening: "Wow, that was a judgment. Again! How interesting." By paying close attention to judgments as they arise, you can get to know what your mind is like when it is judging. What does it feel like to judge? Is it pleasant or unpleasant? What is your body like when you judge? I often experience the feeling of judgment in my belly. Do you feel any stress or tightness? Are there certain judgments that come back all the time? How quickly can you notice them?

remembering the truth of change

In Chapter 5 we discussed the teaching of anicca, or impermanence—the truth of change. If you can remember this truth, you will have a balm for your judgmental mind.

The great sages say, "The only thing that is constant is change." Think how much your body has changed in a few years! Your cells are changing from moment to moment. In fact, I have heard that every seven years, every cell in a body is completely new. Your mind too, changes all the time, from one rapid thought or emotion to the next. Your moods change, as do your view of what is fashionable or cool, your attitude, your longings, hopes, and fears. There is nothing within you that stays the same from moment to moment. The more you meditate, the more you will see this truth about the world.

So when you feel down on yourself, the Buddhist teaching of anicca might remind you that things change. You can't possibly *always* be bad, selfish, or ugly. You will not *always* feel that way. In fact, a lot of the time you are not judging yourself at all, but you may forget this and think a judgmental mind is the norm. Can you notice when your mind changes and judgments are no longer present?

Of course, as you are reading this you may not be feeling bad, so it is easy to think, "Yeah, things are going to change. Duh." But when you are in the middle of a strong feeling, re-membering the truth of change feels nearly impossible! It can take a lot of practice to make the understanding of this truth an automatic part of yourself. Yet, it is possible to know in the mo-ment in which you are experiencing a judgment that *things change.* I have found after years of practice, that when I am caught in a painful judgment, a tiny voice in the background of my mind reminds me "things change." What a relief!

counting judgment

One of my favorite practices is to count judgments. As you go through the day, every time you judge yourself, say "Judging one," then "Judging two," and then "Judging three." Like, "Wow, I got the worst haircut ever! Judging one." "With my luck I'll probably get thrown out of this foster home. Judging two." And so on. If you get to, say, fifty-four and it is only ten o'clock in the morning, you may see clearly how judging is an ongoing func-tion of the mind, almost an unconscious process.

And when you begin to notice hundreds of them, you might soften a little. You might say, "Here we go again! How interesting!" The process of counting judgments may help you to stop taking judgments so personally, and you can see them as they are—merely thoughts that pass through your mind, like gastric juices cycle through your stomach. Can you learn to take them lightly? You might even develop a sense of humor about them. "There is 'I'm too tall' for the ten thousandth time!" As you begin to give the self-judgments less weight, they might even begin to lessen.

the sky is blue

A few years ago my friend Beth was meditating for three months at a retreat center in Massachusetts. In the course of the retreat, she found herself struggling with self-doubt and self-hatred. The voices were torturous! She liked to do outdoor walking meditation in the autumn, when small animals living on the retreat grounds scamper out of their holes to beg for food from the silent meditators.

One day, Beth was walking meditatively outside when a chipmunk popped out of his hole and scurried over to her. As she bent down to feed him, trying to be mindful of her body in the process, he ran away. "I'm such a horrible person," she thought, "Even the chipmunks hate me!"

That day she went crying to her meditation teacher, "I'm so awful, even the chipmunks hate me!" The teacher looked at her and said, "Even the chipmunks hate me, the sky is blue."

Hearing this, Beth relaxed, because in that moment she saw that all of these thoughts were just that, thoughts. There was no actual difference between, "The sky is blue" and "Even the chipmunks hate me." After that, her meditation practice began to change, and she noticed she could be aware of self-hatred much faster and not take it so personally. Frequently she would repeat her new _mantra (spiritual phrase)_, "Even the chipmunks hate me, the sky is blue." It is likely that among your reoccurring judgments is a standout phrase that can rival the one Beth came up with. Like Beth, you can remind yourself that judgements are just thoughts by tacking on to your judgements your own meaningful phrase, or you can use Beth's, "Even the chipmunks hate me, the sky is blue."

judging judging

One last note on judging: please watch any tendency you may have to judge judging. This means, it is easy to get down on yourself for having judgments. "I can't believe what a judgmental person I am!" "I am trying to be kind and all I do is judge people. I'm hopeless!" Judging yourself for judging is like a double dose of something unpleasant.

Since your mind can always find something to judge, the trick is to remember kindness. Everyone judges. There is no one who does not compare him or herself to others. Working with judging is a lifelong task that takes persistence and compassion for yourself. Be aware of judging as much as you possibly can, and always forgive yourself for making mistakes.

We can use the gift of mindfulness to find a presence of mind, and a lightness amid any difficult mind states, especially habitual-

tools for working with judging

- Become aware of judgments. What do they feel like in your body and mind?

- Remember things change. You won't always be that way.

- Count judgments. Notice how many times they occur. They are so normal!

- Add a phrase. A funny sentence can remind you judgment is just a thought.

- Remember kindness. Working with judgments is hard work!

ized thought patterns like judgments. We can work with the automatic judging mind, and soon, with perseverance, we will have an easier time with judgments. Sometimes the self-hatred disappears and we can see ourselves clearly, as if for the first time.

Emily, who began practicing meditation when she was thirteen, made this discovery at eighteen:

> *After practicing meditation for a while, I began to notice those self-hating voices that told me I wasn't thin enough. For years they have been yelling at me. My thighs have been too fat since I was eleven. But lately I have begun to not take them too seriously. The other day when I looked in the mirror and a voice said, "Ugleee!" I just laughed and said, "Hey, you're a voice in my head!" Now I can look in the mirror and actually like what I see.*

exercise: a reality check

1. List all the things you don't like about yourself.

2. Ask yourself the following questions:

   - Have I always been this way?

   - Does everyone perceive me this way?

   - Will I be this way next year?

ten

. . . to being ourselves

In touch with our wholeness,
with a heart filled with love,
there is no such thing as a stranger,
not in ourselves or in others.
In the expanse of true happiness, there
is nowhere for fragmentation to take root
—Sharon Salzberg, American Buddhist teacher

In the last chapter we delved into the painful issue of self-judgment. We learned how to become aware of judgments and to dis-identify from them so as to find refuge from the pain of self-hatred. The positive aspect of this practice is learning how to develop self-acceptance. In this chapter we will take this next step. We will look at the source of self-acceptance, our true Buddha-nature, or inner goodness.

It took a spiritual journey for me to move through self-hatred into a place of self-acceptance. I was in my early twenties when I first got involved with Buddhist practice. Before that I had been a political activist. I considered myself a little wild—I liked to stay up late dancing at clubs in the city and experiment with drugs. I traveled around the world by myself and appeared fearless to my friends. Externally I seemed secure, but inside, like most people, I wanted to fit in, and I didn't think that I did.

I first encountered Buddhism while traveling in India and had a profound sense of "coming home." The teachings seemed to offer hope that I might learn how to be happy, and live a balanced life. I was enchanted with, but also challenged by, meditation practice. When I attended my first ten-day meditation retreat, my mind jumped around like a monkey. I thought for sure it would never calm down. But after struggling for days, completely unable to concentrate my mind, I noticed a shift. Miraculously, I found that I had a little more peace of mind. My mind felt crisp, clear, and balanced. From that moment on I was hooked. I decided to call myself a Buddhist.

I tried to guess at what being a Buddhist meant so that I could be a really good Buddhist. I closely observed the people around me, who were mostly twenty years older than I. To me they seemed "holy." They were quiet and serene, and never seemed to get angry. They never stayed up too late, and were always meditating and reading dharma books. They were generous and helpful. This, I decided, must be what it means to be a Buddhist.

For many years I tried to be my image of what a "Good Buddhist" was. I shut down my opinions and looked to my teachers for what to think. I stopped going to parties and clubs, stopped drugs and alcohol, practiced meditation every day, went on retreats of many months, and explored celibacy. The more difficult challenge was not getting angry. Good Buddhists are not angry people. They didn't seem to be particularly passionate, political, or ever silly. In fact, a lot of them didn't seem to do much of anything, outside of meditating. Yet they knew what they were doing, they were the Good Buddhists, I was the beginner. Fine, I'll be like that. I decided I wanted to meet the standards of the Buddhist world, I wanted to be like everyone else.

Of course many of my changes were healthy and spiritually beneficial. What was not healthy was that I was working so hard at being a Good Buddhist that I stopped being Diana—plain old ordinary Diana, with all her quirks and interesting bits. I gave up my politics, my wild, rebellious, and passionate side. Certain parts of me appeared unacceptable, off-limits.

I had moved to San Francisco, where I spent time with a group of artists who loved to drum and dance and once a year cover themselves in mud and crawl through the downtown financial district. But I wasn't sure I should be friends with them,

how do i become a buddhist?

Reading this book or doing any of the practices described within will not make you a Buddhist. The teachings and practices of Buddhism are open to anyone who is interested, no matter what their religion. Even some people who practice Buddhism prefer not to call themselves Buddhist. However, you may wonder, if I do want to become a Buddhist, how would I go about it? Here are some possibilities:

1. You are likely a Buddhist if you are born into a Buddhist family.

2. If you are practicing at a Buddhist temple and/or with a teacher, you can ask to "take refuge," which means committing to the Buddha (both the historical figure and our own potential to wake up), the dharma (his teachings) and the sangha (the community of followers). After a formal or informal ceremony, you become a Buddhist.

3. You can create your own ceremony, or simply decide for yourself. *I'm a Buddhist.*

they certainly weren't Good Buddhists, they weren't even Buddhist! I was even worried that my stainless steel navel ring with the sky-blue bead stone, which I had gotten that year with these friends, was a sign of heresy. "Buddhists shouldn't be concerned with their body," I thought.

My Buddhist teachers often spoke of the possibility of enlightenment. Enlightenment captured my imagination because it was the pinnacle of the Buddhist path. I decided to pursue enlightenment full time at a traditional monastery in Burma (Myanmar) as a Buddhist nun. In Burma, the pure side of me would be cultivated, and I would be on a fast track to enlightenment as a celibate nun. To demonstrate my commitment to being the best Buddhist I could possibly be, I took out my treasured navel ring. Nuns were not allowed to adorn the body in any way, and in my view, this navel ring wasn't the kind of thing a real Buddhist should have anyway. But my friend Keith put some fishing line in the hole and glued the ends shut, just in case I ever decided I wanted to put the ring back in again.

I flew to Burma where I tried hard to become enlightened. I lived in a tiny hut in the jungle; I ate only before noon; and, except for ten-minute interviews with a teacher every three to four days, did not talk for a year. I spent the entire year meditating, alternating between sitting for an hour and walking for an hour, for up to fourteen hours a day.

I was required to shave my head and wear robes: four layers of salmon-colored cloth, even in over one hundred-degree heat. Snakes and scorpions, centipedes, and giant spiders the size of my hand sent me screaming from the bathroom my first week there. The food often made me sick, and I experienced regular bouts of diarrhea, food poisoning, fear, homesickness, loneliness, and sadness. But no matter what difficult conditions I encountered, I would let nothing stop me, not even snakes! I was driven by the pursuit of my goal: enlightenment.

For the first half of the year I pushed myself, always trying to go that extra mile. I was sure that if I meditated for one extra hour or did walking meditation at an excruciatingly slow pace, then I could break through the prison that made me an ordinary person. I would be transformed into one of the noble ones: an enlightened being.

I pushed myself too hard. Seven months into my practice, I began to doubt everything—myself, the practice, the Buddha's teachings. I could barely meditate. I wanted to go home so badly. Then one day, a dam broke inside me. Self-hatred rushed into my awareness like a great flood. As I watched the hating voices fill my mind, in that instant, I realized I had become a nun to escape what I didn't like about myself, and instead of escaping, the hatred came at me at full force. "What you resist, persists," the great sages say.

In that moment I saw that although I had many good reasons for meditating, underlying it all I didn't much like myself. All my efforts to be a Good Buddhist were about trying to be someone other than me. I had imagined that if I could get enlightened then I would be fully accepted, then everyone would love me, then I would be perfect.

acceptance

I had missed one of the key points of Buddhist meditation practice: acceptance of things as they are. Many Buddhist teachers explain that in order to be mindful, one must have acceptance. I must have been spaced-out when they taught this very crucial lesson.

Michele McDonald-Smith, one of my favorite Buddhist teachers, teaches that acceptance is at the core of mindfulness meditation practice. In fact in order to be mindful of any object in our mind—breath, thoughts, sensations, or emotions, it is absolutely key that we accept the object or experience. That is, we do not try to push the experience away nor do we try to hold onto it; we are willing to be fully there with it, no matter what it is.

Acceptance does not mean passivity. We may try to accept things as they are, but that doesn't mean if, for example, a situation is unjust that we don't try to change it. There is a difference between accepting things as they are and thinking that it is okay for them to be that way.

In our meditation practice, it is not possible to fully be mindful of something without accepting it. For example, if we are experiencing an emotion like sadness, and we think, "sadness is okay, sort of," but really we wish it would go away, we are actually trying to get rid of it, not being mindful of it. Mindfulness doesn't judge an experience. Mindfulness doesn't try to push anything away, nor does it cling tightly to any experience. Mindfulness simply knows what is happening.

The good news is, the more we practice mindfulness, the more this accepting quality of the heart develops. When we make a commitment to practice meditation, this means we meditate no matter what we find in our minds. We may be experiencing boredom or fear, sleepiness or sadness, but we try our best to "just be" with these changing parts of ourselves. The effort to show up and bring ourselves wholeheartedly into the present moment actually develops acceptance, rather naturally. Acceptance is like a muscle that gets stronger the more we use it.

being yourself

All of our meditation experiences happen within our very hearts and minds, and so the more we practice accepting every experience that crosses our path, the more we gain an ability to love and accept ourselves.

In that little hut in the Burmese jungle, I had come to a crossroads in my practice. I had come face-to-face with my own greatest doubts about myself. I could not move forward in my meditation because of the self-hatred. I could have simply quit meditating, gone home or off to sunbathe on the beaches of Thailand, giving up on myself as a failure who wasn't a good enough human being to properly reach enlightenment.

The other possibility was that I could change my perspective—instead of thinking I was messed up and that enlightenment would free me from the things I hated about myself, I could see that those things I hated were actually normal, healthy parts of being a human. I could love and appreciate myself for being me, for being human. I could move forward only by saying I was willing to accept myself exactly as I am. *Then* I could meditate.

I had discovered for myself that self-acceptance was a key to the spiritual path, and includes fully embracing myself, just as I am. I saw it was okay to have preferences, Buddhists are not unfeeling zombies, it was okay to express myself. What was not okay was to think something was wrong with me for a preference I had or a way of expressing myself.

Once I had this realization, I stayed for many more months at the monastery, practicing with an entirely different attitude. Instead of thinking something was wrong with me, I realized that everything about me was fine, in that it was who I was. I was able to practice for the vision of full awakening, without rejecting myself in any way. Each moment became fresh and alive. When I breathed in, being human felt like a gift. My consciousness began to overflow with joy and wonder. "I" seemed less significant. The world seemed to fly by in all its beauty and grace, and I became a grateful participant in the flow of all things.

About a year after I left the monastery, I put my belly-button ring back in. Returning to my ordinary life was not about renouncing my vow to find liberation, but I was giving up the idea that I had to be perfect to do so. Taking out the navel ring had been a commitment to working towards enlightenment. I now saw that putting it back in was, too!

I tell this story with a strong note of caution. Expressing yourself should not happen at the expense of another. The Buddha stressed ethical behavior so strongly because he wanted us to base our actions in the principle of nonharming. He wanted us to live a life that we could feel good about. We will discuss Buddhist ethics in the next section of the book. So although being a Buddhist does not mean denying any part of yourself, or trying to conform to an ideal, it also does not mean hurting yourself or another in the process of being yourself.

If you are on a spiritual path, of course you can be you! Being a spiritual person does not require not having your preferences. You can be a meditator who has a navel ring, or a Buddhist who wears lipstick, or who plays guitar, or who likes punk rock shows . . . The possibilities are endless.

After some years of meditating, seventeen-year-old Mark told me:

> *Recently I've learned to respect my own wish to be happy. I guess when I was younger I had big issues with pleasing people around me, pleasing my parents, proving my worth. Now I realize that I want to learn to live more out of my own needs, being fully myself.*

inner goodness

Spiritual practice will help you accept yourself as you are with your own particular quirks; it will also help you see the Buddha nature within you—the unchanging part of you, beyond all quirks.

Once perspective in Buddhism, a perspective that has proven very helpful to me, is the teaching that we all have Buddha-nature, or inner goodness. Buddha-nature, they say, is the truth of who we are

are. No matter how messed up we feel, we all have goodness at our core. It is our birthright, our true nature. Buddha-nature is inherent in everyone and everything. It is not dependent upon behaving a certain way or being "good" in typical terms. Every person has the potential to be fully awake, and it is already there inside them, not something they have to seek outside themselves. Since goodness is, according to these teachings, the truth of who we are, how can we not accept ourselves—our radiant inner nature?

Sogyal Rinpoche, the Tibetan Buddhist teacher, says,

> So where exactly is this buddha nature? It is in the sky-like nature of our minds. Utterly open, free, and limitless, it is fundamentally so simple and natural that it can never be complicated, corrupted, or stained, so pure that it is beyond even the concept of purity and impurity.

Sometimes it is hard to recognize our Buddha-nature. When storm clouds obscure a bright blue sky, we still trust that the sky is always there behind the clouds. In the same way, sometimes we can't see our inner goodness, yet it is always there. This is what the great teachers tell us. Remembering our goodness is not easy. Trying to remember and live from the knowledge of the bright, radiant nature of our true selves is the work of a lifetime, and we can start right now.

Each of us can directly come into contact with this inner Buddha-nature. You may be aware of a specific way that you already access your own goodness. Elisa, who is fifteen, told me:

> If I'm depressed and I go into the woods, I can't explain it, but a happiness takes over me, and I say to myself, "The trees are here!" And I feel them. And I feel taken care of.

Maybe you feel most in touch with your inner goodness when you spend time with good friends, or when making music or art, or during sports. This feeling may take you by surprise, it can pop up at any moment—walking to the bus stop or taking out the garbage, looking at the rain, petting your cat.

Meditation can be a tool for tapping into the inner goodness. While sitting, we might experience a fleeting feeling that everything is alright in the world. We might sigh and know inside, *Yes, it is all okay. I am good.* This feeling is true self-acceptance, not an acceptance dependent upon anything else, such as other people liking you, or fitting into a certain role. This self-acceptance is based on the truth of our goodness. There are even specific meditation practices that will help us develop love for ourselves and others, as we will see in the next chapter on loving-kindness.

Many enlightened teachers tell us that this inner goodness is the truth of who we are. When we have an intuitive understanding of our inner goodness, self-acceptance is natural. The more we practice, the more we will have tastes of our inner goodness, until we come to celebrate ourselves fully.

exercise yourself

Reflect on these questions and suggestions:

❋ Write down any part of yourself that feels unacceptable to you.

❋ Now write down the thing you like most about yourself.

❋ How is it possible these can coexist?

❋ Have you had an experience of touching into your Buddha-nature? What happened?

❋ Where is it now?

eleven

metta is loving-kindness, a natural joy

> Just as a mother protects with her life her child, her
> only child, with a boundless heart, may I cherish all
> living beings, radiating kindness over the entire
> world.
>
> —Metta Sutta

One summer's night when I was fifteen, I lay back on a yellow blanket in a grassy field. My body had relaxed after a long day babysitting two young children. As I stared at the sky shining brightly with millions of stars, at first a smile, then a warm glow, and then a feeling of bursting joy came over my body. I wanted to laugh out loud because I knew in that moment I was in love with everything on the planet. I began to test myself: Sure I love my parents, my friends, teachers. For a while I recalled people in my life, enjoying the feeling of love and connection that arose with each image, until finally I chose the hardest one. My friend Alexa's brother Jules had been cruel to me. Did I have this feeling of love even for him? I did. I was so surprised but I could feel love for *even* Jules.

The memory of that evening has stayed with me all my life. I didn't know it at the time, but I was experiencing _metta_ (met-uh), a word from the Pali language that means loving-kindness. Although my first experience of metta may have been more dramatic than most, metta is a natural, ordinary quality of a happy mind. Anyone can feel it at any time. Sometimes metta appears and disappears quickly; sometimes it sticks around for a while.

When our minds are not busy with worry, resentment, planning or other preoccupations, we can tap into loving-kindness. Some Buddhist teachings say that metta is the true nature of our minds, the inner goodness that we talked about in the last chapter. Our minds are filled with unlimited, boundless love, but this love is often covered up, making it difficult to experience metta. I like to think of it that way. When I feel metta I sometimes think, "Oh yes, I am experiencing my true spiritual self instead of my busy, ordinary, self-centered mind."

Even ordinary experiences we tend to overlook can be brimming with metta. One of the ways I am happiest is when I spend time with my friends. When we are together, I find myself drawn into their stories, as if I had been right there with them on the occasion they are describing. I feel joy in their victories ("You finally met the person you were dreaming of!"); sympathy when they suffer ("Oh no, I can't believe someone said that about you"). I find myself smiling and laughing a lot. My heart seems to come alive. Sometimes metta seems to bubble up out of me spontaneously for no reason in particular. There is nothing I can trace it to, but there it is, and I want to laugh out loud.

The more I began to investigate metta, the more I saw it as a natural condition that comes from a connection with those we love. It is not necessarily some special experience that is mysterious, magical, or highly spiritual. It is a flowing condition that we can feel when we love our friends, when we are sharing our natural happiness with them, and are tapping into theirs.

Since starting Buddhist practice, I realized that not only is metta a loving quality that can arise in our mind unbidden, alone or with others, it is also a quality of mind that can be cultivated. The Buddha taught meditative practices in order to more fully develop metta in our minds.

the origin of metta

The Buddha first taught metta when a group of monks were practicing meditation deep in the forest. The monks complained that they could not meditate because of the tigers and lions. They asked the Buddha if he could make the wild animals go away. He said, "Sorry, I can't get rid of the animals, but what I *can* do is teach you how to protect yourself with the practice of loving-kindness." He explained to the monks that every single being on the planet wants to be happy and that we can wish them happiness, no matter how frightened or repulsed by them we are. He taught the practice of metta to the monks. After some weeks of practicing, they were no longer frightened by animals.

Some legends say the monks weren't afraid because the wild animals felt the love radiating out of the monks' bodies and refused to eat such kind beings. That may be true. Another interpretation is that with metta in the monks' minds, the monks felt so strong and loving that they automatically felt protected. They couldn't feel separate from these beings, no matter how afraid they were. How could the monks hate or fear the animals while experiencing such intensely loving feelings?

However, I will mention a friend of mine who was practicing metta in the jungle in Burma and found that the bugs, snakes, and scorpions seemed drawn to her! She thought they had "fallen in love" with her because she was emanating so much metta! Because she was squeamish and unhappy, she returned home to meditate in the United States.

I like the story about how metta originated because one of the easiest ways to understand metta is to recall how we feel about our pets. To try it yourself, see if you can bring to mind a pet whom you love. Maybe you grew up with a trustworthy dog or cat. Of course, some of us didn't grow up with pets; in that case, you can bring to mind another animal or a human baby whom you love. What kind of feelings does their image evoke in you? Explore those sensations and see what happens as you notice them. You may get a warm, soft feeling in your heart. You may even start to smile, even as you recall silly or annoying habits they have, like chewing on your shoe. This feeling of unconditional love is metta.

unconditional love

Most of us are used to conditional love. Say you are falling in love with a guy, but you have a sense that you would like him better if he dressed a little differently. You hint to him that you really like boys who wear baseball caps turned backwards. This conditional loving is not metta. With true metta, you are happy with things exactly as they are. Your loving-kindness does not in any way hinge on your object of metta changing themselves, their behavior, or their style to make you like them better. And your metta does not depend on whether or not they return the metta to you.

Have you ever received metta from someone? A grandparent? A close friend? My friend Tempel tried to figure out from whom he had ever received metta. Finally he realized that the one who loved him unconditionally, no matter what he wore, what he said, or how well he performed, was his dog! Between Tempel and his dog existed a natural flow of affection that was not dependent upon Tempel being smart, successful, attractive, on time, or even well-dressed, although he may have been any of those things. When Tempel came home from school in a good mood, his dog jumped all over him, licking him with happiness. If he came home in a bad mood, his dog still jumped and wagged his tail and licked all over Tempel's face. This was true unconditional love (although I suppose some of it depended on Tempel feeding the dog).

understanding metta

In order to understand the concept of metta in a concrete way, try asking yourself, what do you feel like when your mind is filled with love, care, or compassion. Doesn't this feel pretty good? How about when your mind is filled with anger, hatred, or viciousness? For a limited time it might feel good because usually when we are angry, we also feel self-righteous like, "I *should* be feeling this way, I'm right!" But slowly, when self-righteousness fades, we may see how unpleasant it is to be judgmental or angry. Would you rather be right or happy?

Feeling angry or fearful is not wrong. These are normal feelings that arise in our mind. But our fear, anger, or hatred separates us from others. The feeling of separateness is unpleasant—like we are constantly pushing something awful away. Whereas metta is a feeling of connection—like we are binding ourselves to others in the world. We feel joyous, happy, and lighthearted because of this connectedness. Fourteen-year-old Jonah, who learned about metta on his first teen meditation retreat wrote:

> *When I first experienced metta at the retreat during a guided meditation, I felt a wonderful lightness of soul and a great love for everyone and everything. A moving acceptance of myself—a peaceful and calm serenity combined with an almost overpowering joy.*

True metta is a feeling of being at home in the world. No matter how many times our little brother annoys us, we can love him anyway, unconditionally and truly. And we feel that *we* are okay. We can love and fully accept all the complicated pieces of ourselves and others too.

That doesn't mean we necessarily accept all the *actions* of a person. We may try to send metta towards our brother, but feel like he is heading in the wrong direction, hanging out with the

wide awake

wrong crowd. We can fully love him, without assuming he is going to change, *and* we can also suggest to him ways he could im-
prove his life (although he may not listen to us). We can love a
person and not love their actions.

It is also not necessary that we fully understand the object of
our metta. Certainly it is easier to send metta to someone to
whom we feel empathy or can relate to conditions in their lives.
But it is not necessary. We can always return to the Buddha's re-
minder: Everyone, no matter who they are, wants to be happy.

We also have to be careful not to confuse metta with sensual
love or lust. Desiring a person is not metta. Feeling sexual towards a person is not metta either, because in both of these examples, there are elements of attachment—clinging on to a
person, hoping to satisfy some longing. However, we can feel
metta for someone we are physically attracted to, or whom we
are dating. We can truly want them to be happy. Usually we
have a combination of feelings—metta, desire, lust, and conditional love—towards someone we find attractive, or are in love
with. This mixture is completely normal.

developing metta through practice

Metta can be cultivated and developed. Perhaps you have heard it
said of someone, "Oh, he (or she) has such a good heart!" Typically, people assume that humans either are born a certain way
or they are not, that whatever personal qualities they have are inherent. But according to Buddhist teachings, this is not the case
at all. Everybody can develop themselves and realize spiritual
qualities in this life, for themselves.

As the Buddha taught the monks, metta starts with the understanding that every being wants to be happy. Each of us has
the power to wish them this happiness. As we wish others happiness and other good things—safety from danger, health, and a

life of ease, a warm feeling begins to seep into our heart, like the feeling we had when we imagined our pets or a small baby. Often the feeling starts small and grows. In my imagination I feel it spreading all around. Sometimes I see it as a kind of golden light. Sometimes I don't see anything, I just sense it.

We can start by sending metta to ourselves. I imagine the light flowing into my limbs and all around my body. We, ourselves, are worthy objects of metta, and make excellent objects to practice with. We can send metta to ourselves as often as we like and at any time of the day, wishing that we would be safe and happy.

After we have practiced sending metta to ourselves, we can try sending it to people whom we love. We can choose a close friend, or what is called a "benefactor," someone who has helped us at some point in our life. We can pick anyone! A sibling, a coach, a teacher, a counselor. It shouldn't be too difficult to generate metta for someone whose image easily evokes the metta feeling in our mind.

If we wish to, we can expand the circle of metta. When the metta seems to be flowing, we can send it to people we don't know well. Although someone is a stranger to us, doesn't it make sense that they also want to be happy? Even though we don't know the specifics of their lives, we can wish them general happiness, health, safety and peace.

Then if we choose, we can make a radical leap to send metta to people we don't even like—a tricky but wonderful challenge! Even our enemies want happiness. We can notice the difficulty of sending metta to people, on whom at other times we might actually wish unhappiness.

Later we can expand our circle of metta completely and send metta to all beings—human and animals and even all life forms. We can send it to our friends and relatives, to animals, to our politicians, to plants and trees, to areas of conflict on the planet, to our own backyard, to all creatures everywhere, and the earth itself.

metta for the world

I was with a group of teens at a teen meditation retreat and we were discussing the political situation in the world. Particular government policies were making them very angry, and I suggested we try to send metta to people with whom we have difficulties, as an experiment. "Why?" They asked. "Because no one in this world would choose unhappiness over happiness, if given the choice," I replied. I added that, feeling metta in our hearts might be an antidote for the anger we had toward our "enemies." They agreed that this was at least an interesting idea, and worth a try.

We formed a circle, closed our eyes, and then, to get us started, imagined someone we loved was on the inside. We began generating metta for that person. Then I asked the teenagers to imagine putting into the circle someone they had difficulty with: "My brother," someone shouted. "My state senator," said another. "Murderers!" said still another. "No way, I can't send metta to murderers!" another shouted back. "It doesn't matter," I called out, "Keep trying."

The teens and I continued to send metta and after a few minutes it was as if something shifted in the room. We could almost feel the metta pouring out of each of us. Our metta circle began to expand and expand, and getting creative, we imagined "atom bombs" of metta detonating throughout the world. The teens were surprised to find that they could send metta to people with whom they had difficulty, even hatred for. How amazing! One teen later pointed out to me that she realized she could send metta to the person while disagreeing with their actions. I told them of the famous Buddhist proverb: *"Hatred will never cease with hatred, only with love, this is the eternal law."*

what if i can't do it?

Some people have a difficult time practicing metta. No matter how hard they try, that feeling of loving-kindness rarely seems to arise in their mind. Mostly they just feel frustrated. Or rather than love, they might feel anger, grief, or numbness. We can feel like we are failing at this practice if instead of love, we are meditating on its opposite: hatred!

Not experiencing the feeling of metta during this meditation is a completely normal experience, and is actually good news. It means that we get to see for ourselves what obstacles block the flow of metta. As we send our mind in the direction of metta, we can learn what is really happening in our hearts, even if it is painful. Then we can bring our awareness to these states of sadness or aversion, and see what happens as we patiently feel them. The obstacles may dissolve and metta may flow in their place. But sometimes numbness, for instance, is real in this moment, and we don't have to try to change anything. Through metta, we learn acceptance of difficult emotions. In a sense, metta works as a purification practice, helping our minds to gain greater access to the depths of our heart.

So when you are practicing metta and you experience an inability to feel the loving-kindness, simply breathe, notice what is happening and whether you can be present with it, and investigate the experience. Over time, you may notice some surprising changes. And, if metta practice seems too hard, it is fine to choose not to do it.

metta anytime, anywhere

We can have moments and experiences in life when metta spontaneously arises in our hearts and minds. And we have now learned that we can cultivate it through meditation. It is also good to know that we can practice metta meditation at any mo-

ment, any time. We can do it standing in line, in class, in the
woods, at dinner, at our job, even while taking an exam!

My friend Shoshana has been meditating for a few years. Some
months ago she had friends who were on an outside deck at a party
when the deck fell. Nobody was seriously injured, but it was a
traumatic experience for everyone involved. A few weeks later,
Shoshana was at home and she heard the sound of an ambulance
siren, the first thing that popped into her mind was, "Oh no, another deck fell." Then she thought, "That's silly, I don't know what
really happened." In that moment she decided to send metta to
whomever was experiencing suffering from the tragedy, perhaps to
a victim or the family of the victim. Since then, Shoshana has decided to do a practice in which every time she hears an ambulance
siren, she sends metta to whomever was affected by the event. It
has become a regular daily practice for her that she enjoys.

does metta "work"?

When we are sending metta, what, if anything, does the recipient
notice? If we send metta to our mom, will she feel it? What about
someone who is far away? Should we tell people we are sending it
to them? Won't it be disappointing if they don't notice it?

All of these are good questions about metta. I can't offer you
"scientific proof" that metta works, that people really feel it, no
matter where they live. I have heard many stories about Dipa Ma,
an Indian woman Buddhist saint who died in 1989. Dipa Ma supposedly had such a strong "metta-field" that visitors could actually
feel the metta coming from her apartment in the Calcutta slums.
As soon as they came into the vicinity, they felt a warmth and in-
explicably got happy. And supposedly the apartment complex itself transformed when she moved in. Families and friendships
became more loving and harmonious. Neighbors fought less.

I didn't experience Dipa Ma's metta for myself, but this
story indicates metta can have an effect. If you tell people you

are sending them metta, they may feel comforted, whether or not they actually feel the metta. It is wonderful to know that someone is wishing kind and loving thoughts to you. And if they don't notice, no problem, remember metta is unconditional, it is actually not dependent upon getting results.

The one thing I can say for sure is that when you practice metta you will benefit. You will feel a difference in your mind and heart. You will experience a happiness that comes from wishing happiness for others. Your own life will be transformed, because your mind will, at those times, be filled with love and joy. And more instances of spontaneous metta will just bubble up from inside you. More and more you will find yourself wishing even the most surprising people well!

What would the world be like if everyone felt lovingkindness rather than hatred and mistrust towards each other? Much of the world violence would be seriously lessened. Perhaps there would be fewer wars. Metta is revolutionary because if we cultivated it, it could change the face of the planet. Mohandas Gandhi chose to cultivate love rather than hatred and started a nonviolence movement in India that put a stop to British colonization. Martin Luther King, Jr.'s compassionate struggle for justice while loving his enemies brought hard-won civil rights to African-Americans. Both men were ordinary people who knew how to cultivate extraordinary states of mind. Any of us can emulate them. Cultivation begins with each of us. It ripples outwards. Wouldn't metta make the world an incredible place?

exercise: guided metta meditation

Sit in a comfortable position and close your eyes. Check into your heart and see what you notice. Is anything going on in there?

To get a taste of metta, first bring to mind an animal or baby, as we talked about earlier in the chapter. Bring this being to mind; you can visualize images from past experiences with this being, or imagine they are on your lap or in your arms. Notice what happens in your heart. Are you experiencing any kind of love arising? What does it feel like?

Next imagine you are seated in front of yourself. If you can't visualize this well, then just try to get a sense of yourself. Some people like to imagine themselves as a young child.

Try to recreate the feelings you experienced while picturing the animal or baby. You can say phrases to yourself to grow and develop the feelings of loving-kindness, and to wish happiness to yourself: *May I be free from inner and outer danger. May I be happy. May I be healthy. May my life have ease in it* (some traditional Buddhist phrases). If you like them you can repeat them. If you don't connect with them, pick any phrases you want that evokes in you a feeling that you truly want yourself to be happy. *May I be peaceful, may I have good friends in my life, may I do well in school* . . . you choose. Don't pick too many, maybe four or five phrases, and then repeat them.

Notice what kinds of feelings develop in your heart as you say these words. You may feel some joy or kindness, or even forgiveness towards yourself. Allow these feelings to be there and use the phrases you have chosen to encourage them to grow. Repeat your phrases for a few minutes and let the sense of metta spread throughout your image of yourself. If you seem to have lost the feeling, you can always return back to the earlier exercise, picturing your pet or other creature.

Next, imagine a person you love is seated in front of you, maybe someone like a teacher or a relative. Choose someone you respect and from whom you have learned. Send metta phrases to them: *May you be happy, may you be healthy* . . . , or any such phrases of good wishes you choose. Allow the metta to grow in your heart. Imagine that the person gets happier. Do this for a few minutes. Does this help you experience and cultivate more metta?

Then you can send metta to whomever you choose in the world. Imagine friends, parents, relatives, or pets. Follow the directions above, wishing for their happiness. Imagine metta spreading all across the planet, affecting the people, animals, plants, and the earth itself. You can try to send metta even to people you don't know, or even those whom you don't like. Follow your own instincts in directing and sending metta. If you lose the metta feeling, go back to the last person you felt metta for and try again from there, once you have revived the feeling.

You can complement your mindfulness meditation practice with metta. Some people start or end their daily mindfulness practice with five minutes of sending metta. Some do metta when they first wake up or when they go to bed. Some people do it before they eat. Some people even choose to go on long retreats of several months to practice metta.

part four

how do we live our lives?

twelve

it must be karma

The mind is the forerunner of all things. Act with an
impure mind and danger follows thought as the
wheels of a cart follows the oxen that draws it. The
mind is the forerunner of all things. Joy follows a
pure thought like a shadow follows a man.

—*The Dhammapada* (a book of the Buddha's
collected sayings)

Beings are the owners of their karma—or actions.
They are heirs to their karma, originators of their
karma, and are bound by their karma.

—the Buddha

Karma is one of the most confusing teachings in all of
Buddhism. In fact, the Buddha referred to it as one of
the "unfathomables," something so difficult to understand that even *he* could not possibly explain all its details. Once
the Buddha picked a leaf off the ground and then pointed to the
tree from which it had fallen and asked his attendant Ananda
whether there were more leaves on the tree or in his hand. "On
the tree, of course," Ananda, ever the good student, replied.
"Just so," said the Buddha, "That which I know is as many as the
leaves on this tree. That which I teach is as many as the leaves in
my hand." This may be surprising considering how many vol-

umes of the Buddha's teachings have been recorded over the years. Although the Buddha had vast understanding, what he chose to teach was a small portion of what he knew: principles that are relevant to our lives—like the principle of karma.

Karma does not mean luck or fate, as many people think ("Oh, I guess it's just my bad karma that I got a parking ticket," or "It's karma that we met."). The word karma simply means "action," and is usually associated with another not-so-commonly used word (so don't worry if you can't remember it), *vipaka*, which means "results." So, the law of karma actually is made up of these two inseparable parts: actions and the results of actions. Simply, cause and effect.

In Buddhist terms, karma is a law of nature, just like gravity. We can't fight it or try to change it, or even deny it. Karma is not a philosophical doctrine we can argue against; it just is. "Beings are the heirs to their karma," the Buddha said, meaning that no one can escape the results of actions they have done in the past. If we act in a certain way, we will have certain results. If we plant a pear seed, we will get a pear tree. We will not get a plum tree. As it says in the Bible: "whatsoever a man soweth, that shall he also reap." What goes around comes around, as the Rastafarians like to say. With karma, positive actions give positive results. Negative actions yield negative results.

Wait a minute! You are probably thinking, If that's how it works, how come I've gotten away with plenty of bad things without anything happening to me? Or what about when something bad happens to good people, like if the coolest person you know gets cancer?

As I have already mentioned, the law of karma is complex. According to the Buddha's teaching, every time we act, there is a result. But we don't ever know *exactly* what that result will be or *when* we will experience it. The most we can predict is a positive result at some time in the future for positive actions and vice versa. We may, for instance, work hard for years at our bookstore job and never seem to get any kind of recognition, or even what seemed like much personal satisfaction at the time, although we knew it was a good way to make money and become more responsible. But maybe years later we realize how important it was that we were consistent in our job. As an adult we have well-developed perseverance, patience, and determination, although as a teen we wondered whether we were wasting our time.

On some occasions results don't seem immediate because other previous actions also factor in. That is, from time to time we may act harmfully, but all our previous positive actions (even from past lives, some Buddhists say!) help to soften the results. One night we might stay out till three A.M., much later than our parents expected, but since we generally have been trustworthy, we don't get in too much trouble—this time!

At times the result of our actions seem immediate and obvious, as in the mind of eighteen-year-old Jeff, who jokingly called an experience "instant karma":

> *There was this guy on the other baseball team who was always yelling at me. He was so obnoxious. Then his team lost the game, so it came right back at him for being mean to me. Instant karma!*

Of course the effect that Jeff observed (losing the game) may or may not have been directly related to the other guy's behavior toward him. It is possible that the other guy had sowed any number of seeds that would yield negative fruit. But in Jeff's case, it certainly seemed to be a direct result of the other guy's action.

Such examples of "instant karma" happen in everyday life all the time, and they can help us to have a direct understanding of the effect of skillful and unskillful actions. In Buddhist terms, the word skillful means "leads to harmony" and prevents suffering. Unskillful is the opposite. Another way to

do buddhists believe in rebirth?

Many Buddhist traditions stress the importance of belief in past or future lives. When they talk about karma, they might say what you are currently experiencing is the result of previous actions in a long-ago life. For example, if you are wealthy in this life, you were generous in a previous life.

I tend not to stress the teachings on rebirth because there is so much to learn from our current life. I don't believe that waking up in this life requires a belief in a future life. And I don't know, personally, if this is our only life. I don't remember experiencing my previous lives. I have no proof that they happened. However, I don't have proof that this is the only life either. As Voltaire said, "After all, it is no more surprising to be born twice than it is to be born once."

Many people have reported remembering past lives, even under "scientific conditions." Does that make it real? In a way, does it really matter? I like to leave it as the Buddha put it, as an "unfathomable." Besides, I once heard the Dalai Lama say something like, "Act kindly and well in this life. If you are reborn, you will have a good life and if you are not reborn, it certainly didn't hurt to be kind!"

understand karma is to explore how we feel inside and how other people react when we behave with integrity. Having peace of mind (or not!) is a result in itself. Angie, who is fifteen, told me:

One teacher in my school kept making racist comments, right in front of an African-American student in the class. I was really offended, and wanted to say something, but I was afraid he would do something like drop my grade. Finally I couldn't stand it anymore and I spoke up to him in class and then told our guidance counselor. Afterwards a lot of people came up to me and said how glad they were that I said something. I felt good that people supported me and I also felt this sense of relief and happiness for sticking up for something I believed in.

Or, as in the case of Dean, age fifteen, how we feel when we don't act with integrity:

I was skipping school a lot last year. Every day I would leave for school at my regular time, so my parents would think that's where I was going, but then I would just hang out with a friend smoking in his garage. I knew I shouldn't be doing this, and I felt really bad every time I thought about it, but I didn't know how to stop.

We can observe karma directly in our lives by becoming aware of our actions and paying attention to the results. As we bring our attention to these patterns, we will understand clearly what causes harm to ourselves and to others; we will have an experiential basis from which to choose to carry out or to avoid certain actions. This understanding is the foundation of ethical behavior, which we will explore in the next chapter.

influencing karma

Since karma is not fate, we are not locked into a set future. We can influence our future karmic results by how we relate to what we experience in the present—whether that experience is positive or negative, pleasant or unpleasant—and by carefully choosing the actions we take.

If life takes a downward turn, we can get upset and complain, or become self-pitying and feel miserable. We might act in unskillful ways that burden other people and offer ourselves little relief. However, if we understand that a negative situation is the result of past actions, we can choose not to perpetuate the situation. We can say to ourselves, "This is an opportunity for growth. What can I learn about myself from this? How can I change or affect the situation in a positive way?" In other words, how can we take a positive action in response to whatever we are facing, and that action will benefit us, yielding a positive result in the future.

Here is an example: Let's say I am angry because my boyfriend broke up with me. What could I do? I could retaliate with sarcastic comments and casually mention my new love interest. I could plot revenge, or call everyone I know and tell them what a rotten person he is. I could stew in my anger. But do any of these possible actions bring anyone benefit? Do any of them hold the seed for a good result? In the long run, probably not, although they might initially make me think I feel better.

However, since it is my understanding that according to the law of karma, I do have an opportunity in every moment and every situation to create a positive, beneficial result, I might choose to act differently. I might tell him I am hurt, but not blame him for the hurt. I might cry a lot and talk about the breakup with friends in order to gain understanding. I might go for long walks. I might not take it so personally and think about how to move on. Essentially, my direct understanding of karma would support me in acting skillfully.

But how can I choose any of those actions when I am in the throes of anger (or hurt, or despair)? Perhaps I can bring my awareness to the emotions, as I do in meditation practice when I feel discomfort, pain, or strong emotions. When I feel anger rising in my body, I can notice it. I can stop and take deep breaths. I can walk outside of the room and count to ten. I can take a run around the block to avert the initial flow of anger. This does not mean I am pretending that I am not angry, but rather that I am consciously choosing to calm down so that my actions will not flow from anger, producing a result I may later regret. Once I am calm, I can bring my attention to the feeling of betrayal, becoming mindful of it in the way we talked about in Chapter 8. What happens to this feeling as I pay attention? Do I stay angry? What kinds of thoughts accompany the anger? Am I plotting revenge? The thought of revenge is just that, a thought. Then I can ask myself, what can I learn from this situation? I can make a new karmic choice. Although this process may seem difficult or even impossible when we are caught up in strong emotions, wise action in the moment will eventually come more easily.

karma and intention

In the end, karma comes down to intention or choice. Intention is the motivation behind any action we do. According to the Buddha, good intentions will lead to skillful actions and will yield beneficial results, and negative intentions will lead to unwise or harmful actions and yield unhappy results.

We can see for ourselves how important motivation is. Let's say I stepped on a spider and killed it. I could have done this for a number of reasons. I may be disgusted by the spider and want it dead. I also could have *accidentally* stepped on the spider. One act comes out of fear and hatred, the other out of ignorance. Killing the spider would have different karmic results based on the intention behind it. By the same token, lying to deliberately hurt someone or to save oneself from punishment when we have done something wrong, and lying to protect someone else's feelings would have different results, even though the action is the same.

As a Buddhist, one of my core spiritual practices is working to understand my motivations, choices, and intentions. I frequently check in with myself and look carefully at the intentions behind my acts. The more I understand myself, the more I am able to act with the highest integrity possible.

Generally most of us act out of habit on a daily basis without looking closely at why we do what we do. We may, for example, frequently speak badly about our classmates to our favorite teacher. It may feel like we are on automatic pilot, the words just pop out of our mouth without our thinking. But if we bring awareness to our motivation, we might discover that deep down we are jealous of our classmates and are trying to undermine them. When we examine our motivation we can make a conscious choice as to whether or not we want to speak harmfully.

In some circumstances we may be afraid to look at our deeper intentions because they are embarrassing or show us a not-so-flattering self-image. For instance, we might see that we are only being nice to someone because we want to get something out of them, like in fifteen-year-old Bo's case:

> There's this girl I usually ignore, but then I heard she got a car and she lives near to me. Out of the blue, not consciously, I just started treating her nicely. I wasn't even sure why and felt a little slimy about it when she gave me rides home. I know, it's obvious now, I just wanted a ride, but at the time, I couldn't see it.

Checking into our motivations is a courageous spiritual practice. It means we look deeply into ourselves and find out what makes us tick, even if it is embarrassing. Complicating this process is that much of the time our motivation is mixed, which is normal. For example, we may want to join a gang for a complex set of reasons, some of which seem positive and some of which we recognize as negative. Joining a gang might increase our sense

wide awake

of self-worth, give us more friends, help us feel like we belong. And, at the same time, we might want to join because of the rush we get from doing something risky, and we see doors of opportunity we wouldn't otherwise have seen. People rarely have fully positive motivations. We are complex people, and this mix of motivations is what makes us human. Our goal is not to have perfectly positive motivations, but to take the time to investigate and know ourselves. When we honestly understand ourselves better, then we act from a place of clarity. We have a choice whether or not to act skillfully.

And if we look inside and discover something about ourselves that we realize is potentially harming, a bad idea, or against our integrity, we can make a decision not to act based on it. So in Bo's case, once he realized he was treating the girl nicely for selfish motivations, at that point he may choose to stop asking her for a ride, and deal with the unpleasant reality of taking the bus.

acting in or against our integrity

The more we understand how karma and intentions work, the more we spontaneously begin to clean up our actions and act out of integrity. The word integrity means a wholeness and completeness. Acting in integrity means our actions are lined up with our deepest beliefs and we feel whole. One measure of integrity is not, "Do I feel good?", but, "Do I feel good *about myself*?"

Each of us has our own way of expressing integrity. Acting in integrity might mean speaking and acting with honesty, standing up for what we believe in, or acting in ways that don't cause us or another harm. It might mean comforting someone who is depressed, or stopping a dangerous fight from happening. When we act in these ways, we have a sense that we have done something that fits our values and the way we wish to be in the world. Acting against our integrity might mean stealing, or lying, or breaking a promise. It might be treating someone poorly after we have been sexual with them, or turning a younger kid on to drugs. When we act against our integrity, inside, we know we shouldn't have done it, and it does not match our deepest aspirations for how we want to be in the world, but we go ahead and do it anyway.

Acting in or against our integrity can be measured in our gut. We know deep inside us when we act in integrity; we feel it. And we feel it when we act against our integrity. Practice bringing awareness to this "intuition of the body." Developing the ability to recognize being in or against our integrity is one of the most important skills of the spiritual path.

Until we master the art of listening to our gut and bringing awareness to the actions we choose, it might be easiest to see karma in our lives just by noticing the results. Any of us can use our life as a laboratory, observing our actions, examining our intentions, and making a choice to act out of integrity. We may have excellent results, or we may suffer at times. However, as I mentioned earlier, karma is a complex topic that even the Buddha was not willing to fully explain (remember the tree and its leaves?).

Because of its complexity, the Buddha worried people would end up making a lot of mistakes that would lead to suffering. So he offered basic guidelines for behavior. He called these guidelines precepts and said that following them would bring us positive results. The next set of chapters present these precepts with a focus on the areas of speech, drugs, and sexuality.

exercise your karma

Reflect on the following:

✿ When have you seen the workings of karma in your life? When have you acted and the results came back to you?

✳ How do you feel when you act in ways that may hurt people? How do you feel when you are hurt by others' actions?

✳ Can you remember times in your life when you have acted with integrity?

✳ Can you remember times in your life when you acted in a way that was against your integrity? How did you know whether it was in or against of integrity?

Commit to a period of time, perhaps a week, in which you pay close attention to your motivations and intentions. Keep asking yourself "Why?" about anything from small to large actions. Before you watch TV, ask why. Before you drink alcohol, ask why. If you do something you don't feel good about, ask why. If you do something you are proud of, ask why.

thirteen

the five precepts for living

The positive power of virtue is enormous. When we don't live by these precepts, it is said we live like wild beasts; without them, all other spiritual practice is a sham . . . with them, we bring sanity and light to the world.

—Jack Kornfield

The fragrance of flowers of sandalwood
Blows only with the prevailing wind,
But the fragrance of virtue
Pervades in all directions.
—The Dhammapada

Everyday, we are faced with personal choices: *They're passing out Ecstasy at the rave tonight, should I go for it? I really don't want to go on the date with Greg, maybe I should just say I'm sick. Wow, I love that new eyeliner, but I can't afford it, if I took it would anyone know?* And on it goes with endless questions and choices. Sometimes these questions may not seem to be so important, but other times a lot is at stake. How can we make healthy decisions for our lives?

guidelines for living life

The Buddha offered us precepts—"trainings" or guidelines to help us live our lives. These trainings are Right Action and Right Speech from the Eightfold Path, and they are central to Buddhism. In Buddhist countries, even the smallest children are taught and practice the precepts—the ethical guides to living. When I first heard of the Buddhist precepts I imagined that they would be like the Ten Commandments from my own Judeo-Christian tradition. I thought, *Oh no, this is about being a goody-goody. Someone from up high telling me what to do. Don't lie, don't steal . . . give me a break!*

But I was curious. My life felt jumbled, chaotic. I did things I would later regret just because friends were doing them, or because I thought my parents would like it, or because I thought they *wouldn't* like it. I didn't want someone telling me what to do, but I did want a better way to make my own decisions.

It was on a ten-day meditation retreat in Thailand's tropics that I first learned about the precepts. Santikaro Bhikkhu, an American monk originally from Chicago with round, wire-rim eyeglasses introduced me to the precepts as guides of conduct, and a foundation of the spiritual life. He said, "Don't worry, precepts aren't commandments from some authority figure; you won't go to hell if you break them. Precepts are a *practice* and a *training*. You can follow them or not, it's up to you. But you might like your life better if you do."

In a formal ceremony I later committed to the precepts. A Buddhist monk chanted each of them, and I repeated after him. Since then, I try to follow the precepts to the best of my ability while paying attention to the results in my life. I call this my "Precept Practice." I renew my commitment to the precepts every few months—simply by repeating them to myself in a sacred way.

The precepts are not stagnant, ancient rules meant to be recited, holding no meaning for us in the twenty-first century.

They are meant to be rewritten and spoken in ways that make sense to us, so they truly become a living practice. There are many translations of the precepts. The version presented here was inspired by Stephanie Kaza from Green Gulch Farm, a Zen center in California. You can work with this translation or even create one using your own words.

interconnection

I like this version of the precepts because of the first phrase, "Knowing how deeply our lives intertwine . . ." This sentence reminds us that the precepts are based not in judgment and authority but in connection with one another and good common

the five precepts

1. Knowing how deeply our lives intertwine, I undertake the training to protect life. — no killing

2. Knowing how deeply our lives intertwine, I undertake the training to take only what is freely given to me. — no stealing

3. Knowing how deeply our lives intertwine, I undertake the training to protect relationships and to avoid sexual misconduct.

4. Knowing how deeply our lives intertwine, I undertake the training to speak truthfully and kindly.

5. Knowing how deeply our lives intertwine, I undertake the training to protect the clarity of my mind through avoiding intoxicants.

sense. We say this phrase to remember that our actions affect
one another. We are not living in isolation, but on a planet
where, as the physicists say, even the beating of butterfly wings
ten thousand miles away can change our weather patterns.

We may seem separate from everything else, but we would
not be here if it weren't for thousands of people, animals, plants,
and the earth itself. Think about it, we are only here because our
parents (who were conceived by their parents) conceived us.
Their parents were conceived by their parents, and so on . . .
Our parents or other adults took care of us since we were tiny,
helpless babies. The food that sustains us comes from others who
grow and harvest vegetables, beans, grains, fruit . . . somebody
else packaged and shipped these crops . . . the plants grew because of the sun and the rain . . . our clothes come from plants,
animals, and synthetic materials, clearly from the labor of other
humans. The precepts are founded on this fundamental Buddhist
teaching, which is acknowledged not only in spiritual, but also
scientific, circles: We are all interconnected.

the five precepts

Keep in mind as you read, over time, you will develop your own
relationship to the precepts. I will tell you what the Buddha laid
down, and you can reflect on them, explore them in your own
life, follow them if you choose, and observe the impact in your
life. Later you can make decisions about whether they become
guidelines to live by. As we will see, the precepts are very rich
and complex, so they can become a practice of a lifetime.

First we will look at these precepts from a personal perspective—how they work in our life, and then examine them
through a lens to think about larger problems in the world.
Some Buddhists feel we do not have to think so widely about the
precepts. Others feel it is important to see how far-reaching
these precepts can extend.

interconnection

We are all connected to one another and all things exist in dependence upon all other things. As Thich Nhat Hanh says, "In this grain of rice I can see the presence of the entire universe." See if you can experience the truth of interconnection for yourself:

As you are looking at this book, allow your mind to imagine where this book came from. The paper came from trees, but what conditions were needed for the trees to grow? The sun, the rain . . . Who made the paper? Where does the ink come from? The outside cover, the binding, all of these were made by humans and machines. How were the machines made? Where do these humans come from? What have they needed to live? For five minutes let yourself imagine the webs of connection, as far back as you possibly can.

1. Knowing how deeply our lives intertwine, I undertake the training to protect life.

This first precept is the basis of all the other precepts: avoiding harm. The first precept means to undertake, as a training practice, not to take life. Buddhists give up intentional killing and avoid unintentional killing.

Depending on where you live, not killing humans may seem more or less relevant. For some people, handguns in lockers, drive-by shootings, and gang violence are a fact of life. Making a commitment not to kill and to protect life could be a powerful act amidst a violent environment. Others from different backgrounds may not experience this level of violence daily, and say they would never consider killing a human, but what if they had to defend themselves? The Buddha would say that even in self-defense one must not kill. In Buddhist teachings, this precept also extends to not taking our own life.

The Buddha also opposed the killing of any life form, no matter how small. He asked his followers not to hunt, fish, or kill any kind of animal whatsoever, even for food. Following the precepts, one couldn't even "put your dog to sleep," even if the dog were in tremendous pain. The Buddha even said not killing applied to insects such as ants and mosquitoes. How amazing we get so anxious and frightened that we want to kill a bug that is one-millionth of our size! Not swatting an annoying mosquito may seem absurd, yet this is the Buddhist guideline; we each have to decide what makes sense for our lives.

What about indirect killing—receiving the benefit of something that has been already killed? This is very tricky. In the Buddha's time, monks were not allowed to eat any food that had been directly killed for them, although they were still allowed to eat meat if it had not been killed for them. What about wearing fur coats or leather shoes? What if the leather jacket wasn't killed for you, but you bought it at the mall? Does your shopping contribute to further killing?

The need to kill—no matter whether human, animal, or insect—is generally out of anger, revenge, or frustration, or because we feel we are the most important life form and that our existence comes before anything else. Is this true? When we kill we forget the truth of interconnectedness. According to Buddhism, all life forms are equally important and dependent upon each other.

This first precept can be understood not only as not killing, but also as doing our best to protect all life, from the forest to the oceans, to our own backyard. We can explore the precept further to see whether following it would mean we oppose and actively work against the death penalty and war. Some Buddhists believe they must become conscientious objectors if they were drafted into the military. In my own practice, this precept guides me in opposing nuclear weapons and other instruments of war. I ask, how can I protect the earth and all of its life forms?

2. Knowing how deeply our lives intertwine, I undertake the training to take only what is freely given to me.

This second precept is usually translated as not taking what hasn't been given, or not stealing. Traditionally, any kind of robbery or theft was prohibited. So shoplifting or stealing of any kind would break the precept.

Almost everyone takes some small things that haven't been offered. For instance, you might take something from a friend's house on occasion, like grabbing a magazine that you are sure has already been read. It is just a magazine, but it wasn't really yours for the taking. Even subtler might be borrowing clothes or CDs from a friend and forgetting to give them back. Other kinds of stealing might include cheating on a test, copying answers from someone next to you, or plagiarizing someone else's words for a paper. Some of us may struggle with shoplifting.

I try not to take anything that belongs to other people or hasn't been genuinely or freely offered to me. Sometimes whether it has been offered is unclear; it might be offered to me and I don't know it. So I make sure to always ask first and not take it, even if I *need* it. I don't even "borrow" shampoo when I am sleeping over at a friend's house. I always ask first. Sure, shampoo is not such a big deal, but I am very interested in that state of mind that thinks I deserve something.

When I feel like I deserve something, a voice in my head thinks that I am important. It thinks I am more important than the other person from whom I am taking the object. Objectively, we all feel that our happiness is important, we deserve to be happy. But in Buddhism we believe in the truth of interconnection. And according to this truth, I cannot truly be happy if someone else is suffering, particularly if I have caused their suffering. Check this out for yourself. When you take something

that belongs to another person and you realize that person will
be upset, can you fully enjoy the taken object?

In the Second Noble Truth, the Buddha said that attachment
causes suffering. Stealing often happens when we are attached to
an object, stealing is the extreme result of wanting something.
Learning not to take things, develops the quality that is the opposite of attachment: renunciation—letting go of things. The Buddha spoke highly of this wonderful spiritual quality. Renunciation
is a quality of mind that can be happy by fully accepting whatever
it has. It doesn't need anything outside itself to be happy.

The important aspect of this precept is the sense of safety it
creates. When someone never "borrows" something from others,
we feel safe around this person. We trust him or her with our
things, our secrets, our time. When someone is trustworthy he or
she creates an atmosphere of safety that people want to be around.

On a more global level, this precept can be interpreted to
mean not taking *anything* that hasn't been offered. This would
include appropriation of land from native peoples, and taking labor or resources from one country and using it for the economic
benefit of another. There are many instances of stealing on a
global scale, although rarely is it called stealing.

*3. Knowing how deeply our lives intertwine, I undertake the training to
protect relationships and to avoid sexual misconduct.*
This precept may be of particular interest to you, so I have devoted all of the next chapter to exploring the issue of sexuality.
Briefly, this precept is about taking care not to engage in sexual
misconduct; that is sexual activity or use of our sexual energy in
a way that could harm ourselves or someone else. Traditionally
this precept refers to avoiding sexual activity with anyone who is
in a committed relationship.

Since sexual activity is an area of our lives that can cause a lot of
pain, we can understand why the Buddha made a precept about
sex. People hurt others through sex. Cheating on someone is a sure

way to harm a relationship. Being cheated on is incredibly painful. We can even use our sexual energy to harm others, such as flirting with someone we have no intention of following through with, or using the promise of sex to get something we want.

Simply put, this precept is about doing our best to protect the safety and integrity of relationships. It is about respecting commitments—our own and those of others. Exploring this precept in your own relationship may require you to ask yourself if you have created safety with your partner. Does it feel right to engage in sexual relations if you or your partner is not "ready"? When is it right to become sexually involved?

A fuller exploration of this precept might include the ways in which we can work to protect children from sexual abuse and even to prevent sexual abuse in the culture at large. Would the use of sex in advertising be considered harming? We might question whether the pornography industry breaks the precept and what might be our responsibility towards the exploitative industry.

4. Knowing how deeply our lives intertwine, I undertake the training to speak truthfully and kindly.

Chapter 15 is a full exploration of wise speech. In brief, this precept invites us to speak truthfully, kindly, and with awareness. Another phrasing of the precept asks us to refrain from false and harmful speech. In Buddhist terms, harmful speech is any speech that is harsh, dividing, or meaningless.

For most people, truthful speech is one of the hardest precepts to follow. This is primarily because when we are unaware, we easily say whatever pops into our heads at any moment. Most of us are not trained to be aware of our speech. Lying can cause a lot of damage—to others and, of course, to ourselves, as we spend time trying to cover up lies or making sure we don't get caught. We all know how bad it feels to be lied to. The feeling is usually much worse than having been told a difficult truth.

Harsh speech is speech that is rude, cruel, or abusive. Again,

wide awake

180

this is a kind of speech that can harm, and is often rooted in a lack of awareness or in unchecked anger or hurt. When we have awareness of our speech, we can choose to hold back our angry words until we have calmed down a bit and can convey the same point without trying to hurt the other person. Kind speech also invites us to have gratitude and appreciation for life and the people in it.

Dividing speech is when we speak ill of one or many people in order to divide them from another person or group of people. Dividing speech can break couples or groups of people apart, and can be extremely painful. Harmonious speech brings people together, resolves conflict, and is in service of the good of the community. Idle speech is meaningless speech used to fill in gaps when we are afraid of silence. It is speech that has no purpose. Meaningful speech comes directly from our deepest parts of who we are. It connects us to people and the world.

As we explore the speech precepts, we may ask ourselves where speech is false or harmful in the larger culture. Would following the precept involve standing up for freedom of speech and opposing censorship?

5. *Knowing how deeply our lives intertwine, I undertake the training to promote the clarity of my mind through avoiding intoxicants.*
This precept concerns not clouding our minds with drugs or alcohol and we will explore it further in Chapter 16. In committing to this practice, we avoid intoxicants that make our judgment fuzzy or confused, or simply covers up our own inner wisdom and good judgment. Some Buddhist teachers argue that if one uses drugs or alcohol, one is more likely to break some of the other precepts, such as stealing, lying, or harming with sexuality.

Most Buddhist traditions encourage us to abstain completely from drugs as they lead to "heedlessness." Heedlessness means acting without awareness. A few Buddhist teachers are slightly less strict and ask followers to judge for themselves the impact of intoxicants on their body and mind. Might one drink or joint be okay occasionally? As I have described, each of us must come to our own understanding and comfort level with these precepts; they are meant as guides not absolute truths. However, no teacher I know of thinks that alcohol or drug use is a good idea.

Some people suggest this precept might also apply to non-drug intoxicants such as excessive TV watching, computer use, or even unhealthy eating. All of these activities cloud and confuse the mind. Too much of anything can be a problem! This precept invites us to cultivate respect for the sacredness of our bodies and minds.

One may ask whether working in the alcohol industry, or even bartending or serving alcohol would break the precept. And if we choose to follow this precept, would we be committed to larger societal issues such as working against alcohol and drug abuse?

three levels of precepts

Our relationship to the precepts may shift over time. We will likely experience this shift as three different levels:

First, we hear about the precepts just as we might hear about any other ethical "rules" and we agree to adhere to them because we understand intellectually that they are the right thing to do. Perhaps an authority figure strongly "suggests" we follow them and we don't want to get in trouble for breaking them.

On the next level, we begin to see results in our life. *Wow, if I tell the truth, people rely on me more. If I stop lying, I have more friends. Hey, my meditation practice seems stronger when I'm not worrying about getting in trouble for stealing that nail polish.* At the second level of working with these precepts, the results make sense.

The third level is when we begin to embody the precepts automatically; they become who we are. You may hold some of them already. One fourteen-year-old boy I know, new to hearing the

"are buddhists vegetarian?"

The Buddha did not actually preach vegetarianism. He was a wandering monk and lived off donated food, whatever it was, whether vegetables or meat. Monks set out each morning on an "alms round"—walking barefoot, carrying their bowls, and receiving food from the villagers or city folk, or visiting villagers' homes for meals.

In some Asian Buddhist countries, vegetarianism is an important part of the spiritual life. In most Asian Buddhist countries, people also eat meat. High altitudes in Tibet, for example, make it difficult to grow vegetables.

The bottom line for Buddhists is the first precept: giving up intentional killing and avoiding unintentional killing. So if you did not kill or order the food killed, you are sticking to the first precept. This is, of course, a simplistic or "convenient" way of looking at things. Many choose not to eat meat for a variety of reasons— political, spiritual, health-related, and ethical.

Some Buddhists feel that fish, poultry, and cattle are living beings, which should be protected. Whether or not killing was done explicitly for the person eating the animal, killing occurred. Therefore, they refrain from eating meat. Other Buddhists are concerned about factory farming, and the cruel ways in which livestock are raised. Still others care about the forests being cut down to provide grazing land for cattle, or the huge amount of grain that is used to feed livestock while humans starve.

precepts, said, "I would never imagine stealing anything. I just couldn't, it's not me." For others it is not that easy. The third level means we don't have to work at it or even think too much about it, precepts come naturally, like with sixteen-year-old Sean:

Honestly, I don't think I've ever intentionally killed a mosquito since I was fourteen and went on my first teenager retreat. We learned about the precept not to kill, and they asked us to notice how often we want to kill bugs. I decided to stop killing all insects, just to see what that's like. Now, it's so integrated that I'm not even noticing the change in myself.

messing up

If you decide to try to follow the precepts, be prepared: Everyone messes up some of the time. Committing to the precepts does not mean we will never do harm. Sometimes I tell white lies, and I have "borrowed" things belonging to others. We cannot decide to stay locked in our room for fear of stepping on bugs. Undue caution is a misunderstanding of the precepts.

The precepts are not about already being perfect; they are considered practices. We will make mistakes, learn from them, forgive ourselves, and then start over. We call it "practice" because we are *practicing*. We try to follow them and observe where we break them and learn from those mistakes. And we don't judge ourselves for messing up. We may feel disappointed or remorseful, but then it is important that we start again.

My friend Aran, who has been meditating since he was sixteen, described it perfectly to me:

When I meditate and my mind wanders off the breath, I try not to get mad at myself. I just start again in the very next moment. It's the same with me and the precepts. I break them sometimes, but I try not to get mad at myself. I learn

working with the precepts: cheating

Sometimes we unintentionally break precepts. Everyone does it. However, when we deliberately break them we have a perfect opportunity to get to know ourselves better. We can go inward to learn why we did it, and if we are honest, we may learn some surprising and insightful things about ourselves. The process for working with the precepts is simple: *If you break a precept, ask yourself why.*

When I was working on this chapter, I was flooded with memories of precepts I had broken as a teenager and had forgotten as an adult. I remembered that in high school I sometimes cheated by looking at answers the class math genius had written on her calculus tests. Cheating is not explicitly one of the precepts, but is closely related to the second, which rejects stealing, and the fourth, which promotes truthfulness.

I knew that I wasn't supposed to cheat, nevertheless, I did it. Ironically, I didn't even *need* to cheat; my grades were already good. I did not have the precepts to help me consider whether cheating was a good idea or not. I only had a general sense of morality—"shoulds" told by my teachers and parents. My sense of integrity told me it was wrong, but a part of me didn't care.

Had I ever been caught, I might have reflected on what had ever possessed me to cheat. I might not have spent hours trying to figure out how to avoid the consequences. But had I observed the precepts when I was sixteen, whether I had been caught or not, I might have noticed that I was breaking a precept and I could have asked myself why. If I *had* asked, I might have learned that I was putting enormous pressure on myself to do well in school. I was terrified of not making straight A's, and of disappointing my teachers and parents. If I had been honest with myself, and learned this, I might then have talked with the school counselor about my need to be perfect. Some guidance in high school might have made a big difference in my later life. Instead, I kept cheating, without reflecting on my behavior and my underlying motivation.

In a way, the precepts are like *catching ourselves* rather than waiting to be caught, or worrying about being caught. We catch ourselves and this develops our inner compass. Asking why we broke a precept, not beating up on ourselves because we did, and reflecting deeply on hard issues, teaches us maturity, responsibility, and gives us a deeper understanding of who we are.

getting results

As I practiced with the precepts, they created a safety net for me. People started to trust me more. They knew I would not deliberately hurt them. They trusted me with their secrets, and with their belongings. Once at a party a friend said, "One of the things I like most about you is that you're so ethical. I really trust you." How often do we receive compliments like that?

Over time, the precepts got more interesting. I discovered where I had problems I didn't have the courage to admit to. When I want to break the precepts, I notice how *important* I feel ("I deserve that soap!"). I now take a lot of joy in this process. Here's something new about myself!

I also noticed a change in my meditation practice over time. I saw what my meditations were like when I kept the precepts, and what they were like, before, during and after breaking them. When I first started meditating, I obsessed about unskillful things I had done when I was younger. For instance, during one long meditation retreat many years ago, I spend a whole week feeling guilty about stealing doll clothes when I was twelve from a girl I babysat for. I could not stop thinking about the stolen clothes fifteen years later! These days, I have less worry and remorse when I meditate because I am holding the precepts more strongly than when I first started.

the bliss of blamelessness

The more I began to clean up my act, doing my best to practice with the precepts, the less worry I had in my mind. I didn't feel guilty since I was no longer doing things that were in conflict with my sense of integrity. The practice had led to a clarity and strength of mind. What sweet relief! It wasn't as though I was trying to be good. It was that I began to like myself more and more as I followed the precepts. I felt a confidence in myself and my actions. Suzanne, who is eighteen, put it this way:

> I see the precepts as respecting self and other, paying attention to what feels right, and not being harmful.

Before I left Thailand, the monk Santikaro taught me one more thing I have never forgotten. He told me about the "bliss of blamelessness." He said, "When you act in ways that are in sync with your heart and no one can fault you, you feel happy, blissed out. Imagine living in a way that can not be chastised. No one says, I don't trust you. Why? Because you *are* trustworthy. People respect you. You respect yourself. This feels very good. Think of your effect on the world." He was right.

exercise your precepts

1. If it is possible, go out into the woods during bug season. Commit to one hour where you will not kill any bug. Sit or walk around, and as the bugs attack you, become

aware of your emotions, your frustrations, your desire to kill, and just notice what you can. What happens when you don't kill? What do you observe in your body and mind?

2. Decide that for one month you will not take anything you are not sure does not absolutely have your permission to take, even the littlest thing like a glass of water. What happens when you do this?

3. For one week, observe how you experience your sexual energy, and how you relate to people sexually. Do you act in any way that might potentially hurt another?

4. For one week, as a practice, do not say anything that you don't know for absolute certain to be true. For instance, if you have heard some news but you haven't verified it personally, don't repeat it. Observe what happens as you try this practice.

5. Think about what intoxicant you have difficulty with. Maybe it is a drug or alcohol. Maybe it is computer games or television. Vow to not cloud your mind with this intoxicant for one week. Observe the results.

fourteen

sex

Aware of the suffering caused by sexual misconduct, I vow to cultivate responsibility and learn ways
to protect the safety and integrity of individuals,
couples, families, and society. I am determined not
to engage in sexual relations without love and a
long-term commitment. To preserve the happiness
of myself and others, I am determined to respect my
commitments and the commitments of others. I will
do everything in my power to protect children from
sexual abuse and to prevent couples and families
from being broken by sexual misconduct.

—Thich Nhat Hanh

Have you been waiting for this chapter? Did you skip to
it? Are you dying to know what the Buddha has to say
about sex?

Well, of course you are interested in this chapter. Nearly
everybody is curious about the subject. In the United States, and
other places in the world, people are preoccupied with sex. Sex
is used to sell everything from cars to deodorant. The plots of
films, music videos, and TV shows revolve around sex. Humans
spend a great deal of time thinking, worrying, and obsessing
about sex. Some worry because they are not in a sexually inti-

mate relationship; others who are involved are equally concerned about that.

Exploring our sexuality and various kinds of sexual activity for the first time can be terrifying. We may not be sure how far we want to go, or how to stop if we begin to feel uncomfortable about possibly having gone too far. Some friends may be having sex and telling us we should try it too. Some adults may be telling us not to have sex at all. We may not even know for sure whether we are straight, gay, or bisexual.

When we are ready for the experience and have an appropriate partner, we can have extraordinary moments of closeness and intimacy through sex. Yet, if we act without integrity, we can also hurt people through our sexual actions, too.

The Buddhist teachings can help us make sense of this confusing area of our lives. Sex can be a place of spiritual growth when we bring our practice to it.

sex and sexuality

First off, I want to distinguish between sex and sexuality. We all have to deal with our sexuality, whether or not we are having sex. Sexuality is a general term meaning everything from our sexual identity to our hormones and the changes they are causing in our bodies. Sexuality includes our emotions, desires, and the instincts that relate to our bodies, sex (the act), and love. The word "sex" is even confusing because it can be comprised of sexual activity of many different kinds, including intercourse. So sex is the range of physical acts, sexuality is all the broader issues, including our sexual energy.

sexual misconduct

Many of the Buddha's followers were ordinary people who practiced the dharma in the midst of their daily life. The Buddha did not suggest that lay people (as nonmonastics are called) practice celibacy—no sex—like monks do, but he provided lay people with a precept in regard to sex. The third precept is translated as "no sexual misconduct," or, not harming through sex. The traditional understanding of this precept is to not have sexual relations with anyone who is married or in a committed relationship. I prefer to expand the interpretation to not using one's sexual energy or activity in a way that could cause harm to oneself or others.

Following this precept, in its broader sense, requires conscious awareness and skill. Because we receive so little guidance about sex, and so much negative input from the popular culture, sexual misconduct is virtually a rite of passage. Almost everyone I know has, at one time or another, hurt others through their sexual actions. When sex is scary and new, we may be so caught up in the emotions around it that we don't think about consequences. A large percentage of those in supposedly committed relationships have either cheated on their partner, or been cheated on. One partner or both, or even others, like friends or parents, can get hurt.

At times some of us can even be deliberately hurtful. If we are not paying attention, we may not be aware of what we do. We experiment, try things out, are frequently confused, and often we act without thinking about the consequences, like twenty-year-old Annie reflected:

the third precept expanded

Knowing how deeply our lives intertwine, I undertake the training to protect relationships and to avoid sexual misconduct; that is, avoid sexual activity or use of my sexual energy that could harm myself or others.

My best friend was bisexual and she also had a big crush on me. I really loved hanging out with her—she was so smart and funny—but I was not attracted to her in that way, and sometimes I felt a little uncomfortable and even guilty about that since she obviously really liked me. I had been sexually active with boyfriends, but wasn't in a relationship and started to wonder whether, if she was attracted to me, maybe I was really gay and didn't even know it. So one night I was at her place and drank a lot of wine and went to bed with her. I didn't like it and I didn't want to do it again. She felt like I used her and it ruined our friendship. This was a year ago and we aren't really friends anymore and I miss her. I feel bad because I know I really hurt her. She really loved me.

I like to include "sexual energy" in the definition of sexual misconduct, in addition to sexual actions. We can easily see how we hurt people through our actions. Less obvious is how dishonest intentions and misdirected energy can hurt people. But they can. For instance, sometimes even our flirting can backfire, as fifteen-year-old Jocelyn found out:

I was flirting with this guy at the beach party. I didn't like him or anything, but he was so into me that I just kept flirting because it felt like such an ego stroke. He was hanging on my every word. I knew he had fallen hard for me, and I had to break the news that I just wasn't into him. You should have seen his face. He was totally pissed off and really hurt, I realize now.

non-harming

When I think about the opposite of sexual misconduct, what *right* sexual conduct means, I think non-harming. As with any of the precepts, here too, avoiding harm is the bottom-line of my life and the Buddhist philosophy. When I am hurtful to people, the memories of past painful actions and their consequences circulate through my head. I feel unsettled, remorseful. When I am non-harming, I feel more alive, more connected to myself and others, and more at peace.

If we feel confused about a particular action, we might ask, *Could this result in someone else or me getting hurt?* Sometimes we don't know, of course, but I believe it is always best to err on the side of caution. *Well, it might hurt Lou if I sleep with Jo, then again, she might not care at all. But maybe I should play it safe.*

As we are human beings, we sometimes cannot escape hurting each other, but we can still hold a deep intention to make non-harming our bottom line, and hold to it as perfectly as we are able. As we discussed in the karma chapter, we can try to be as aware of our motivations as possible to avoid hurting others and ourselves. I can't stress enough the importance of getting clear about our motivations, as sixteen-year-old Lee saw:

Shana, my girlfriend, wanted to have sex with me. I thought I was "ready." I'm seventeen. Everybody else is doing it. I told her, give me a week to think about it. During that week I kept asking myself why and I realized that the main reason I wanted to do it was because I was afraid she'd think I wasn't cool enough if I didn't. In truth, I wasn't ready and that seemed like a pretty stupid reason. I was glad I saw how I really felt and, yeah, we stopped going out because she couldn't deal with me saying no.

And sometimes we find if we closely look into our motivation, we may not like the reasons for what we are doing, nor the activity itself. Tanio is eighteen and just started college. Every few months he came to the young adults Buddhist group. One day the group was talking about sex and he said, "Oh yeah, girls are hot, I go for whoever I can, whenever I want it. I don't care about her, I just want as much sex as I can get." All the other teens in the group questioned him. "Why do you do that, Tanio? Girls are people too, they don't exist just for your pleasure. How would you like to be talked about that way?" He left the group sulking. A few months later, he came back and said he had been thinking about the way he acts sexually. He was embarrassed, but admitted that deep down he didn't feel good about himself:

> Girls liking me helped me to feel better about myself. I realized how ridiculous I had been and now, I don't know, somehow I feel ready to do things differently.

celibacy

For monks and nuns, the Buddha prescribed celibacy—abstaining from all sexual activity—and there are good reasons for this. As I mentioned before, sex takes up a lot of our mental energy, and physical energy, of course.

If you have ever committed to an intentional period of celibacy in your life—for example, if you have ever decided that you won't date until after the big test or big game, then you know, other things take on more importance. You can focus more singlemindedly on your art or music or school work, or whatever you choose. This is what Liz discovered for herself at nineteen:

> I made a vow that for six months I wouldn't have sex with anyone. It was really hard at first but then it got easier and I saw how much I think about sex! During this time I began to take dance lessons and soon I was devoting most of my energy to them. I am now thinking of becoming a professional dancer.

Buddhist monks and nuns give up sex so they can devote their lives to spiritual practice. This does not mean that they do not *think* about sex. When I lived in the monastery as a celibate nun for a year, I thought about sex plenty. But I had made a commitment that my meditation practice came first. When I shaved my head and wore robes that concealed my body, I felt I was nobody's idea of a sexual object. I could relax and focus my energy solely on meditation. When sex fantasies came up, I would remind myself what was important this year. I felt protected by my celibacy. No one stared at me or harassed me in ways they had in the past.

Of course my experience was limited to a single year. Monks and nuns who commit to a lifetime of celibacy have permanently given up sex, but they still have their sexuality to work with. They still experience desires, hormones, and instincts. Rather than act on their instincts, they channel their sexual energy into their practice. Monks and nuns who commit to celibacy find this element of their spiritual practice challenging but rewarding.

We can learn a lot from practicing celibacy even for short periods of time. Illana and Jared met on a five-day teenage meditation retreat. Right away they were very attracted to each other. They had agreed to follow the third precept, which requires celibacy on retreat, but still there was a lot of sexual tension between them and they resented the limitation they had agreed to. On the last night of the retreat, they went off into the woods. They sat together under an outdoor gazebo, and stayed up late into the night talking. They spoke about their families, their interest in spirituality, their questions about meaning in life, and how weird it was to follow a precept about sex. It was one of the deepest conversations either of them had ever had. Suddenly they shared an insight. It was *because* of the precepts that they were able to get this deep. Had they been at home they would have already been sexual, when they didn't really know each other yet. They would not have spent all night talking. The precept, they recognized, actually helped to protect them and improved their friendship!

am i ready for sex?

At some point everyone faces the big, important question: Should I have sex with that person? In the quote introducing this chapter, one of my teachers, the Vietnamese monk Thich Nhat Hanh suggests that intercourse without loving, committed relations is sexual misconduct. Another teacher, the British monk Ajahn Amaro, recommends you ask yourself: If one of us accidentally got pregnant, would I want this person to be the parent of my child? These are both valuable gauges. We can also ask ourselves, Does this sex make *both* of us happier? And of course it is important to look at issues of safe sex— prevention of STDs (sexually transmitted diseases) and pregnancies.

If you are considering sleeping with someone, take a realistic look at that person. Do you want an ongoing committed relationship with them? Do you even want them to be your friend? You might decide that if you don't want to be friends with a person, then you don't want to have sex with them either. Pressure to have sex can be strong, especially when lots of your friends are doing it. When we have sex and we don't feel ready, we can end up feeling used, unworthy, or confused, as sixteen-year-old Tara experienced:

I don't even want to talk about the time I had sex with Paul. We were in the back of his car. I could tell he basically didn't care about me, I was just a conquest. I wasn't even sure if it was date rape, I mean, I agreed, but I didn't really want to do it.

Learning to check in with ourselves about what we want, a practice this book has been teaching, can be invaluable. What does our intuition tell us? It is fine not to have sex. One friend of mine has a dating rule: he wants the sexual intimacy he has with someone to be equal to their emotional intimacy. If the person

barely knows his mind—his secrets, his thoughts and feelings,
then he will not let them know his body.

Does this make him a prude? Not at all. It shows that he is tuned in to how he is affected by sex. Sex has the power to hurt us on a much deeper level than we care to admit. A lot of us are numbed out emotionally. Numbing out doesn't mean we are not affected by something. In fact, the opposite is more true. We have numbed out because we are so affected that we can't stand it, so we shut down. We would rather not feel.

If we are committed to waking up, we will not be able to live a life numbed out or disconnected from our inner experience. Through "Right sexual conduct" as an integral part of our practice, we become more aware of ourselves, more tuned in to others, more deliberate in our actions and more aware of our underlying motivations. The point of this precept, as with the other four, is not to regulate behavior, but to live life more consciously.

awareness and sex

And when we are ready—emotionally, physically, and spiritually—for sex, we can practice awareness there too! Applying conscious attention to sexuality is a wonderful, though advanced, practice. We can practice being aware as we touch or are touched by our partner. What is it like to kiss someone and know that they are absolutely present and not thinking about kissing someone else or about basketball practice? Sharing all the sensations and opening to the often intense emotions together is an incredible experience. We can feel ecstatic. Sometimes fear arises. Sometimes we feel joy. Sometimes we are transported somewhere else, or have a mystical sense of union.

When we are sexual without awareness, that is, if we rush and space out, we miss this kind of thing. I am referring to being conscious. Use your time together as an opportunity to understand yourself and your partner more deeply. Can you even be conscious in the middle of difficult emotions that might arise? Chapter 8 offers some tools for working with strong emotions.

If we are slow and careful and aware, even holding hands can be an extraordinary experience. See what happens as you begin to develop more awareness through your meditation practice. See if you can apply the same level of awareness when you are sexual with another person.

our own sexual ethics

Taken together, the precepts are excellent guides for making choices about how we will act. Ultimately, each of us has to make our own choices for our lives and develop our own code of ethics. We can arrive at our sexual ethics in one of two distinctly different ways. One way, for example, is to make a conscious decision: "No intercourse until I am in a committed, loving relationship." This type of decision will be based on what we think will best help our lives, or what people we respect have told us. Making a decision about sex in this way, while not easy, is straightforward and is less likely to be fraught with perils.

The other way to arrive at our own sexual ethics is to bring the rules of practice to sex. In meditation practice, we try hard to be aware, but may only be able to keep our mind on the breath for one minute out of a whole hour. But if we are serious about our practice, we don't accept that as the best we can do and give up. We keep trying, and learn from the instances when we space out. In the case of sexuality, doing something that leads oneself or others to feeling numb, hurt, or shut down, is obviously a departure from the intention of the practice of waking up. We might want to reflect on the motivations that led to that action and decide that we might not choose to do the same thing again. This path of trial and error is the more difficult path, because almost inevitably the process includes pain. But on this path, we will gain a direct understanding of the immediate results of our actions, and learn to make choices based on this wisdom. Ultimately, we will embody our own sexual ethics: It will be part of who we are.

Please be gentle with yourself. Sexuality is a powerful area of our lives, no matter what our age. There is a tendency to act irrationally, and stray from our deepest intentions, especially in the heat of the moment when we are turned on by another person. Something else takes over! Thanks to the urgings of our hormones, we are probably going to make frequent mistakes. That is okay, but we will have to face consequences—the results of our actions. All we can do is keep trying to act, with as much awareness and integrity as possible.

sexual identity

Can Buddhists be gay, lesbian, bisexual, or transgendered? In contemporary Buddhism, it is accepted that you can be attracted to and love people of your own gender. Buddhists come in all shapes, sizes, and certainly sexualities. The Buddha did not dwell on issues such as whether it is okay for men to be sexual with men or women with women. His main concern was the ways in which unchecked, unaware sexuality can be harmful. Your sexual preference is a personal choice, relative to a host of factors including genetics and culture. The same guidelines about sexual misconduct apply if you are heterosexual or homosexual.

exercise your sex ethic

Reflect on these questions:

❋ Have you ever unintentionally hurt anyone through your sexual actions or energy? What was your intention? Where did you go off course? What was the result? Have you done the same thing again?

❋ Have you ever been hurt through someone else's sexual actions or energy? Were they intending to be hurtful? How did their actions hurt you?

❋ In either case, how did you feel?

❋ What is your personal sexual ethic?

If you are in a relationship, talk with your partner about what he or she would need to increase the feeling of safety in the relationship. Ask each other what would feel protective of the relationship. What would break the relationship's trust?

fifteen

wise speech

> Abandoning harsh speech, he or she abstains from
> harsh speech, he or she speaks such words as are
> gentle, pleasing to the ear, and lovable, as go to the
> heart, are courteous, desired by many and agree-
> able to many.
>
> —Majjhima Nikaya, 179, Buddhist text

Have you ever had a best friend tell you she doesn't want
to be friends with you anymore? Has your coach yelled
at you for something you didn't do? We feel the effect
of these words deep inside, they seem to rebound in our bodies
for hours. And yet these are only words, "small mouth noises,"
as one friend used to say.

With language, we can either heal or hurt. We can tell
someone we love them, or that they must be crazy to think we
ever found them attractive. We can provoke anger with words,
or with a few choice words of praise, we can send someone into
a state of bliss. Much of the time we are barely aware of the
power of our speech.

Since words do have so much power, mindfulness of speech
is a particularly important and powerful practice. However,
even those who have been practicing Buddhists for twenty years
or more will say that this practice remains a challenging one.

Luckily, the Buddha provided some guidelines that can keep

Knowing how deeply our lives intertwine, I undertake the training to speak truthfully and kindly.

us oriented. The guidelines are grounded in the first of the precepts: not harming. They are also an expansion of the fourth precept: the commitment to speak truthfully and kindly. How do we avoid harm in our speech?

four kinds of unwise speech and their opposites

The Buddha spoke of four areas of speech that were harmful to others and ourselves: harsh, dividing, false, and idle or trivial; and he recommended four kinds of skillful, helpful speech, the opposites of harmful speech: kind, harmony-producing, honest, and useful.

harsh versus kind speech

The Buddha asked followers of his path to refrain from harsh speech—aggressive, rude or cruel speech. When we speak harshly, our underlying intention may be to hurt a person. We might say something nasty in order to get back at someone, because we are angry at this person, or even because it feels good to treat someone meanly.

Generally, harsh speech springs from a lack of awareness. We might snap out of anger or frustration, and harsh words come flying out of our mouth. Or we are upset about something unrelated to the present situation and we verbally jump on a person because we haven't taken a moment to separate the two situations. Sometimes harsh speech can be especially painful when exacerbated by drugs or alcohol, as fifteen-year-old Toby experienced,

> *My mother has a drinking problem. Sometimes when she is drunk, she grabs me and shouts about two inches away from my face: "You make me sick, you are disgusting!" I go into a tune-out mode because I would fall apart if I let the words sink in.*

Harsh speech even includes nonconstructive criticism, such as telling a person in a critical way what is wrong with them or something they have done.

Cursing unnecessarily also falls into this category of harsh speech. Frequently we swear because we are trying to be cool, or because we are copying someone we respect. Sometimes it makes us feel superior to speak harshly. Notice how this kind of speech tends to build up our ego.

The Buddha's recommendation to speak kindly is simple. Be as kind as possible with our speech, or at least be careful of being unkind. Think of how we feel when someone speaks to us in a

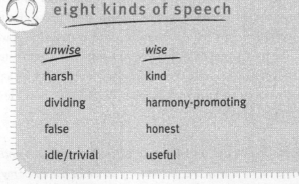

eight kinds of speech

<u>unwise</u>	<u>wise</u>
harsh	kind
dividing	harmony-promoting
false	honest
idle/trivial	useful

truthfully loving way. The Buddha asked us to consider the type of relationships we wished to engage in—loving or hateful. He knew that kind speech promoted harmonious relationships, which he saw as a significant part of the spiritual life. Cruel speech can rip relationships apart.

Of course, there are times when criticism is necessary and helpful. A rule of thumb might be, could we say what we intend, but put it into a positive light? Can we criticize the behavior, as opposed to the individual? Can we express how their behavior makes us feel? We might say, "When you don't show up on time, I feel upset that I can't trust you," instead of, "You jerk, you're never on time! Why do I hang out with you?"

As you may have guessed, the Buddha's antidote to speaking harshly was awareness. The Buddha asked us to be as aware as possible of our thoughts and emotions, so that we could prevent harsh speech. When we are aware we can notice the impulse to be cruel in our speech, or we can notice when we are preoccupied with other worries so that our speech becomes accidentally rude or hurtful.

When we read the Buddha's suggestion to speak kindly, we might feel that we have to be fake nice. The Buddha did not ask anyone to be fake. If you remember, he spoke strongly against lies, so any fakeness would be contrary to his teaching. He was not trying to turn people into goody-goodies. He simply wanted us to understand the harming and healing potential of speech.

One excellent practice is learning how to express gratitude and appreciation on a regular basis. Most of us take for granted people like our parents and friends, but someone's self-esteem can be transformed simply through hearing kind words on a regular basis. Sixteen-year-old Juanita discovered how loving speech helped her:

At least once a day my boyfriend tells me he loves me and then he tells me why, like, he likes my sense of humor or my approach to schoolwork. Sometimes he tells me how I have helped him, like, I'm pretty relaxed around getting into college so it makes him less stressed out. I love when he tells me he loves me and means it.

dividing versus harmony-producing speech

Next the Buddha asked us to refrain from dividing speech— speech that creates separation or alienation, or can break groups or couples apart. This kind of speech is very common, particularly in politics these days. It would be very unusual for opposing political candidates *not* to promote their platform by speaking ill of their opponent. In this case, using speech to divide people is a way of gaining power. It is a painful process to watch the governing parties of one nation speak in a dividing way about other nations. One government creates fear and hatred towards another nation and thereby gains support within its own country.

Pitting nation against nation is ironically much like behavior in high school. Those of us still in high school can experience a power rush from using speech to divide groups of people. We can feel a sense of righteousness and control. Yet dividing speech can be incredibly painful for those who are divided. Groups, friends, boyfriends and girlfriends, all can have their relationships severely harmed by this kind of speech.

Dividing speech often occurs when someone feels bad about him or herself. It is a common tool of people whose relationships are breaking up. One partner is angry and hurt and announces to their friends all the terrible things their ex did. They want people to stop liking their ex, so their own hurt feels somehow avenged. Having a nasty conversation about some of your friends with another friend in the same crowd, thus causing your clique members to turn against each other, would be another example of dividing speech. Fourteen-year-old Diane saw how painful and confusing this kind of speech could be:

*My friend Mary is always talking about how I am her best
friend and how Brenda is a loser and we should all hate her,
but act like we like her when she is around. Then I found out
she was saying the same thing about me to Brenda when I
wasn't around. I couldn't believe it!*

The Buddha asked that we choose our speech to be harmonious, or to cause harmony. He encouraged speech that sought to bring groups together. He was known as a great reconciler, and was able to stop wars in India by virtue of his wisdom and kind words. Imagine speech so powerful it could end wars!

The Buddha invited us to explore the sense of power or righteousness we get from speaking ill of one person to another. We can look at our motivations behind dividing speech— whether it is low self-esteem or hurt feelings, or even the rush of power. He asked us to examine the kinds of communities and relationships we wished to see flourish in the world. And whether the feeling of self-importance is worth the pain it brings to others.

One example of harmonious speech is when two friends are in a fight and we talk to each of them separately, encouraging them to listen to each other and forget their differences. Whether or not we are successful doesn't matter. The two may never get along; but our speech was skillful and we attempted to reconcile. One young man found his life's work—preventing conflict and bringing about peaceful resolution in his inner city school:

*They call on me when bad arguments and fights start in the
high school. They know I can help because five years ago
when I went to school there, my best friend shot another
friend over something really stupid, they got into an argu-
ment and couldn't work it out. After that I realized I had to be
the one to stop fights, no one else was going to do it. Now I
teach teens when they get angry to be careful of their words.*

*I teach them to try to move towards peace rather than vio-
lence. The lesser person is the one who says the stuff that's
gonna lead to violence.*

lies versus truths

The Buddha cautioned against telling lies. Many of us struggle
with lying. The Buddha explained that lying leads to suffering.
He was not being judgmental; he was simply pointing out the
results of the action and encouraging truthful speech as a wise
way of life.

For some of us lying is not a chronic problem. But for others, lying is habitual and often doesn't seem to have a good reason behind it, like Jake, who is seventeen, admitted:

> *I caught a fish and said it was fifteen inches, but it really was
> twelve inches, I'm not sure why I said it, but I just did.*

Usually, however, lying causes some kind of suffering, even if it
is about little stuff, as fourteen-year-old Tina told us in meditation class:

> *I sometimes lie about little things, like I tell my teacher that I
> left my homework at my other parent's house. The worst,
> though, is when I really do leave it there, and then I feel it's
> too late, like I wasted my excuse. I'm like, no really, I did
> leave it at her house!*

Recently one teen pointed out to me, "It was a major thing
to lie a hundred years ago, now it's really common, everybody
does it. It's an accepted part of our culture." I think she has a
good point. Lying is endemic in the United States (and perhaps
many other countries), as evidenced by the plots of TV programs and films, and by the stories in the news media. I know
many people who say they can't trust anything they read in the

newspaper, or hear on certain radio stations, or on the TV news. We might think, why should I tell the truth if everyone around me is lying? We might wonder how we can know what is really going on in our world if we can't get unbiased, honest news? Some feel the Buddhist precept of not lying also means that we need to address lying on a mass level in our culture. It may mean that we take on the cause of freedom of speech and information, and work against censorship.

Although there are always a few instances in which a lie was intended to save or protect someone else or for a higher good, usually when I lie, I am trying to protect myself. I am afraid of some consequences or hurting someone's feelings, or I feel lazy or unmotivated, and a lie may serve to get me out of a task I find unappealing. Lying seems easier than telling the truth. For example, I don't want to finish a project, so I say I lost it. I don't want to hang out with a friend so I say I am sick. The truth may be that I am having difficulties with this friend. If I were honest then maybe the two of us could work on the problem between us. Instead, I lie because I am fearful of either hurting her or dealing with the growing pains of changing the relationship.

Sometimes lying makes us look better, smarter, more "with-it." How about those little lies, like exaggerations. "I saw that movie fifty times." Did we really have to say that? It is interesting practice to notice when we exaggerate and ask ourselves why we did it. Often we may be surprised by the answer and may learn something about our need to be recognized, or seen, by others.

The bottom line is we are lying because we can't be present with the truth. We are afraid in some way. We fear a particular type of suffering so we avoid that suffering by lying. However, often we find that what we have to do to avoid the truth has far worse consequences than if we had told the truth in the first place. If you have ever had the experience of telling a lie and then having to tell another lie to support the first lie, and so on until you have created a complex story you can't even remember, then you have had a vivid experience of the way more suf-fering is created by lying.

The Buddha placed a high premium on honesty. Being truth-ful at all times takes great courage and is an ongoing, challenging spiritual practice. We can work on it every day. I have discov-ered that the less I lie to others, the more I can be honest with myself, and vice versa. Honesty allows me to go deeper inwards to understand myself because I am not protecting myself or locking myself out from any part of my psyche. I am willing to be present with all parts of me. One friend who was working with this practice said,

> *I am dedicated to knowing the Truth, but how can I know what is Truth if I lie to other people? When I lie to other peo-ple, I get confused inside about what is really going on inside me, and then I can't make space for real Truth to come to me.*

Telling the truth does not mean that we tell *everyone every-thing* all the time. The Buddha also asked us to consider "appro-priateness" and "timeliness" with our speech. Just because something is true doesn't mean it is useful or appropriate. It also doesn't mean it is the right moment to say it. We do not *need* to lie, but we also do not need to say whatever comes to our mind. Or we may need to wait a while before we can say something without it being hurtful, or until the person can hear us better.

idle versus useful speech

The Buddha's fourth guideline is refraining from idle speech. Traditionally, in Buddhist monasteries, any speech that wasn't about the Buddhist teachings was considered idle. Of course that is not terribly realistic for us in a life outside a monastery.

Sometimes I reflect on all of the times I open my mouth and speak for no reason at all. Maybe I want to fill an uncomfortable silence. Maybe I don't want people to think I am boring or weird. Most of the time I speak out of habit, and certainly, constant speech is conditioned by our culture. Noise surrounds us all the time, as if people are afraid of silence. The newspapers, TV, and radio are filled with gossip—about celebrities from politicians to entertainers. Is all this noise useful, worthwhile, beneficial? Seventeen-year-old Latonya described the impact of idle speech on her:

> I have a friend who talks non-stop about whatever comes into her head. It's like she pushes the "on-button" and says anything she wants, no matter who is listening. She drives me crazy and I can barely stand to be with her anymore. But she is one of my oldest friends, so I don't know what to do.

Another form of idle speech is gossip. Gossip can seem like a lot of fun. Most everyone loves to hear about and tell stories about other people's lives. But more often than not, these sto-

Gossip

Gossip is talk for no good reason, usually with an intent to share information about another person, generally someone who is not present. To gauge whether your conversation is gossip, ask yourself whether you would say these words about them if that person were sitting in front of you. If I wouldn't make certain remarks or comments to a person's face, it may be best not to say it at all. Check your motivation. Take a moment and reflect on gossip. What state of mind does gossip evoke? How do you feel afterwards?

ries dwell on other people's difficulties or misfortunes. Unfortunately, gossip is like eating a giant meal of sweets and junk food—potato chips and Twinkies. It may taste delicious going in, but a little while later we feel nauseous and wish we had kept our hand out of that bag or away from the wrapper. I try to remember how I feel afterwards when I am about to gossip. Not gossiping is a spiritual edge for me—not easy!

The Buddha encouraged useful speech—the opposite of the blah, blah, blah that plops out of our mouths. I like to view this guideline as a request for "deep" speech—meaning, about important topics that we care about, rather than anything that zips through our minds. Dean, who has worked hard with this speech practice since he was fourteen, had clear and obvious results:

> *My friends say I am one of the deepest people they know. I can make anyone talk about issues that are really important to them, because that's what I care about. I don't want to waste my time talking about garbage.*

Sometimes it is useful to share stories about what our friends are up to. And at times it can be helpful to discuss another person with a close friend if we are trying to sort things out such as this person's relationship to us or an action of theirs we find confusing.

In such situations, it is important that we check into our motivations. Are we talking about someone with the intention of making them look bad and us look good? Or do we want to clarify information or share news—Antonio and Joo Eun are dating! Or are we trying to understand a situation and need help from another person? Fourteen-year-old Robin saw how speech could be helpful:

> *When I was fighting with my girlfriend, my best friend, Shantila, was great. We could sit for hours and discuss what was going on. I don't think we did it in a mean way. She was just trying to help me, and it made all the difference.*

Sometimes checking our motivation is difficult. Motivation is often mixed; it may be partly positive and partly negative, or it may not be obvious even to ourselves. But checking into our motivation can be a practice for us: "I really want to tell the story I heard about Sean and Louise, but why do I want to? Hmmm . . . I guess because I would never do something like that and I want people to know I look down on it . . . Hmmm . . . Maybe I should keep it to myself."

Frequently, I have to remind myself that I am not perfect. I am engaged in a practice with my speech. If and when I lie, or gossip, or speak harmfully or divisively, then, as with the meditation, I start again. I can take some time to reflect on the negative consequences, but I don't harangue myself over them. We are all human!

Wise speech is not about being a goody-goody. A lot of people like to joke around and make wisecracks. Some people feel that their speech would be pretty boring or even fake, unnatural if it were only wise speech. Some of us might have a sense of humor that leans toward irony or sarcasm. Is it okay to joke divisively or to lie as a joke? These are questions that we can each explore on our own. We can consider our motivations for telling a particular kind of joke. We can notice our feelings about the way our humor is received. We can consider whether anyone was harmed by our joke. We can see for ourselves and understand the harming and healing power of speech.

communication from the heart

As we practice with these guidelines, we will learn to "speak from the heart." Speaking from the heart involves checking into ourselves—connecting deeply inside with what is important to us, and speaking with honesty and depth. At times, our words may feel like they come from a mystical, wiser part of us. The more we practice, the easier and more spontaneous speaking this way becomes.

We can also learn to listen from the heart. Listening from the heart is being fully present for whatever we are hearing. When we are with friends we can practice awareness, listening carefully and considering everything that is being said, not spacing out or thinking about our biology test or the cute guy in math class. We can try to give everyone the full attention that we would like to have given to us. This wonderful story came to me from an eighteen-year-old named Jorge who had almost never talked about his parent's divorce:

> *After Chris's dad died, late one night we got in his car and drove around for hours telling stories and crying. It was one of those really clear nights, you could see every star, and we drove and drove and he cried and I talked about my dad splitting on our family and I can't explain, but it was like there was something holy between us. He understood me better than anyone in my life, ever.*

When I meet with teens all over the world, sometimes I bring a "talking stick" to use in talking circles or councils, to remind us to speak and listen from the heart. A talking stick is used in native people's ceremonies around the world. The stick is passed from speaker to speaker around a circle. When we hold it, we are reminded to speak with depth and honesty. I found my talking stick in the forest in New Mexico outside Los Alamos Nuclear Laboratory of nuclear weapons research and development fame. The nuclear waste from the laboratory, the by-product of fifty years of experiments, is currently stored in giant tanks in various designated areas throughout the nearby forest. Although the labs say the forests have never been contaminated with radioactive waste, the forest is in danger of this terrible desecration. So I have taken the stick and I use it in circles with teenagers. It is a metaphor for using our speech to heal the planet—what I see as the ultimate benefit of right speech.

exercise your speech

✳ Practice observing your speech. Of the four unwise kinds of speech, is there one you do all the time? Is there one you never do? Do you keep your word to yourself? How wise is your speech on a day-to-day basis? Don't try to change anything immediately, just gather information about yourself and your habits.

✳ During the course of a week (or a month . . .), choose one day when you vow you will not speak harshly, another when you will not speak in a dividing way, another when you will not lie, another when you will not speak frivolously. You can plan it in advance or choose when you get up in the morning. Spend the day observing what it is like to make these commitments. Is it hard? Easy? What do you learn? You will likely mess up, but don't worry about it, observe what happens as you practice with it.

✳ You can choose to take on these commitments for longer periods of time—several days, a week, two weeks, and so on. What happens in your life?

wide awake

sixteen

protecting our bodies and minds: working with intoxicants

All beings are unclouded from the very beginning,
but the haze created by drink and drugs prevents
them from knowing this.

—Robert Aitken, Roshi, American Zen teacher

We have all heard the "Just say no to drugs" rap. Personally, I am not today a big fan of intoxicants—drugs and alcohol—although I experimented a little with them in high school and college, mostly because everyone else was doing it. When I was drunk, I felt more at ease in social situations. Other drugs made me feel creative and visionary. I was lucky because I never formed a habit of any kind. When I became serious about my meditation practice, much of what I had been looking for in drugs and alcohol became available to me through my meditation. I found myself more confident in social situations. I could more easily access my natural creativity and visionary capabilities. In essence, I had found a new way to get high, one that over time has proven far superior to intoxicants.

So what did the Buddha say about drugs? Is it time for another "say-no-to-drugs" rap?

Truthfully, the Buddha was opposed to intoxicants. He was in favor of developing compassion, wisdom, and an awakened mind. He felt that intoxicants interfered with our spiritual development and made our minds more cloudy and confused. The fifth precept, which he taught to his followers, invites us to protect the clarity of our minds through the avoidance of intoxicants. The Buddha did not compromise: he simply forbade drug and alcohol use.

avoiding intoxicants

Contemporary Buddhists interpret the fifth precept in different ways. Some Buddhist teachers, strictly following the Buddha, say under no circumstances should one use drugs or alcohol, as they divert spiritual seekers from their path to awakening. These teachers strongly believe that drugs can cloud our mind and cause us to act in harmful ways. They recognize that even drug use done at first in the spirit of exploration or discovery, can lead to addiction. We may become dependent and give away our power to these substances. Mostly these teachers are concerned that our perception becomes distorted under the influence of drugs, and we might act in ways we otherwise wouldn't. For example, when we drink, we are less aware, and it becomes more likely that we might break any of the rest of the five precepts. We might lie, steal, or become sexually intimate with someone with whom we know we shouldn't have.

One of my teachers, the Vietnamese Zen master Thich Nhat

the fifth precept

Knowing how deeply our lives intertwine, I undertake the training to protect the clarity of my mind through avoiding intoxicants.

Hanh, suggests that since alcohol abuse is so widespread and underlies so much societal violence—rape, spousal abuse, murder, as well as crime in general—a personal stand for a Buddhist who cares about the world would be to absolutely say no to alcohol. If you think it is bad for society, is it okay for you?

That is the hardline stance on drugs from the Buddhists.

Another consideration in regard to intoxicants is how they affect our spiritual practice. During periods of committed spiritual practice when we are trying to understand and focus our minds, drug use is prohibited. When I was a Buddhist nun, and at other times when I attended retreats, I was asked not to take any substance. But the truth was, I didn't want to. I was making discoveries about my body and mind that were far more interesting than any entertainment or revelations I could have had with drugs. Compared to the amazing insights in my meditation practice, drugs have largely paled in comparison.

Each person will have a unique relationship to drugs and alcohol. For some of us, not doing drugs comes easily. Some teens may never be interested in drugs, but may feel pressure to do drugs, and feel left out of the "cool group" or even made fun of if they don't join in the partying, as Ron, who is fifteen, found out:

The first time I tried smoking pot it just made me dizzy and nauseated. I've never done drugs since then, and I'll tell you, being one of the few people in my school who doesn't use is a sure way to be unpopular.

Others feel intrigued and compelled by drugs, yet see that in the service of their growing spiritual practice, it might be useful to try to use less. For some, stopping drug use may not necessarily be the way they want to live permanently, but may be useful to experiment with for a period of time, particularly when they are developing their spiritual lives.

not confusing our minds

There are other Buddhist teachers who are a bit more lenient, and translate the precept as "not doing drink or drugs that cloud or confuse the mind." The distinction is largely a matter of quantity, that is, how much one can drink and still have a clear mind. But in some cases it may be a matter of a particular substance for which individuals have a tolerance. Unfortunately this interpretation is vague and can be unclear. How much alcohol or drugs is enough to cloud the mind? Is an occasional glass of wine or a joint once a month a problem if it barely clouds the mind? Is drinking a beer now and then okay? I cannot answer these questions for you. Your relationship to drugs and alcohol is your own. For some of us, a little bit now and again doesn't seem to be a problem, and may not affect our clear thinking or our meditation practice. For others, one beer could lead to an addiction.

"Not using intoxicants that cloud and confuse the mind" is also practical advice—if we can look at drugs objectively and clearly, exploring how they affect us. If drug use causes us to feel mentally cloudy and confused, and we find ourselves acting out of this confusion, then we know for ourselves that we don't want to keep using the drug. We may find that we much prefer our mind off of drugs. Our mind may feel clearer, wiser; we may feel more fully ourselves. Unfortunately, with this method of decision making, our judgment may not be clear enough to tell whether or not we are confused!

Clearly, the surest choice would be to avoid intoxicants altogether. For those who already habitually use some kind(s) of intoxicant, avoiding them may require a radical life change. It may mean breaking with groups of friends or being left out of your usual social scene. It may even bring you face to face with underlying pain that drug or alcohol use had been masking. For those with a major addiction, quitting may require Alcoholics Anonymous or working with a therapist or counselor. I realize stopping

drug use can take determination, strength of character, and a
daily recommitment to that intention.

am i avoiding something?

I am interested in the way that drugs can be used to check out of
life—helping us to disappear from the difficulties we encounter.
Certainly we all confront countless problems. We face our parent's
divorce, a friend's suicide, an unwanted pregnancy, a breakup.
Who wants to feel these kinds of pain? Adrianne told me,

> All through high school I was smoking pot. I thought it was
> because it was cool. Everybody did it, especially the kids in
> my "crunchy granola" crowd. I was smoking pretty much
> every day and it wasn't even affecting my grades too much.
> Meanwhile my parents were fighting all the time, my sister
> was sick, and I hated myself. It was only a few years later that
> I realized my life was a mess and I was smoking because I
> didn't want to feel how bad I was really feeling all the time.

Unfortunately as we face these difficulties, few of us have any
kind of mentor. Some have minimal support from our parents,
teachers or even our peers for working with these problems.
And at the same time, we receive societal messages, including
countless media images glorifying alcohol, and the message that
our difficulties can be avoided. We often observe adults—and
even our parents—avoiding their problems, coming home to
that beer, martini, glass of wine, or joint each evening. Humans
use intoxicants to check out of life because intoxicants have
proven over time to be wonderfully numbing. When we ingest
alcohol or smoke marijuana, we feel spacey and zoned out, or
relaxed and peaceful. Our problems "stop mattering." On some
kinds of drugs we may feel "completely in control," or as if none
of our problems could touch us.

Directly facing the pain of our lives takes tremendous courage. We can make a spiritual commitment not to run away from any part of our life, no matter how difficult. We can choose to avoid intoxicants, not because adults continually tell us that they are harmful, but because we have made a commitment to waking up in our lives and acting from integrity. We can avoid them because we have concern, based on experience, about what goes into our bodies and how our minds are affected.

nondrug intoxicants

Drugs and alcohol aren't the only intoxicants. There are many time-honored ways to check out of life and avoid facing our pain. Many of us spend hours in front of the TV, computer, plugged into a Walkman, or immersed in nonstop busyness—work, school, social life. This incessant activity is a nondrug intoxicant that also clouds and confuses the mind. I have found that when I spend a lot of time absorbed in the Internet or TV, my mind feels disconnected and spacey. And my mind gets jammed with ads, commercials, and often sexist, racist, or plainly ridiculous "information."

Even the individual events in our lives can produce an intoxicating effect. Our minds and bodies are the storehouses of all we ingest and experience. One event, like being asked out by the person of our dreams, can reverberate in our mind for days, and stay within us at a deep, almost cellular level, distracting and affecting us. Sometimes we are conscious of its effect, sometimes the impact is below our conscious awareness. If we spend time in silence, we will see for ourselves how we are so easily affected by what we take into our bodies and minds. My friend Karim told me,

> When I was younger I loved horror movies. I craved that terror and the adrenaline feeling in my body. I even liked the gore. Years later in meditation, the movie murders I had wit-

nessed replayed in my head for hours, and I was sick to my stomach for a week. When I asked myself, do I want this in my head? the answer was unquestionably no. So I stopped watching these movies.

Because everything that goes into our bodies and minds affects us, paying attention to what we choose to consume is important. Going cold turkey—that is, completely quitting every kind of intoxicant in our life—may not be necessary, but may also make sense at times. The Buddha talked about the Middle Way—finding the place between excess and abstinence.

psychedelics

Often when the subject of drugs comes up, someone points out, "Not all drugs are the same." They want to distinguish from other intoxicants drugs that many consider to be "mind-expanding"—the psychedelics, otherwise known as hallucinogens. In this category are drugs that have been used throughout history by various cultures for sacred purposes—peyote, psilocybin mushrooms, and some would include marijuana, and even tobacco. In more contemporary times we have also seen LSD and its various chemical spin-offs, and in the last couple of decades, Ecstasy (MDMA)—the visionary or "love drug."

So, what about drugs that arguably don't "cloud or confuse the mind," but perhaps can provide insight into ourselves? What about drugs that allow us to "see God" or more fully expand our consciousness? These are important questions.

Yes, drugs have been used in ceremony and for healing purposes throughout human history, particularly in native or indigenous cultures. Unfortunately, few ritualistic contexts or sacred ceremonies for drug use still exist these days, as our contemporary society is so secular—so removed from any sense of the sacred.

It is apparently true that some drugs have helped people to have psychological insights, visions, and healings at times. But most teens don't use drugs in this controlled, ritualized fashion. Generally, psychedelic drugs are associated with partying.

And yes, there were the legendary sixties. A lot of people (who now are *in* their sixties) were spurred on their spiritual search with psychedelics like LSD. Many seekers tripped on acid or mushrooms and found themselves encountering a realm of mind and spirit far different than anything they had ever before known. Some people "saw God." Others melted into a union with all things in the universe. Others felt like they finally "understood everything."

In broad terms, all of these are spiritual experiences, and many who had such experiences were eager to find ways to incorporate them into their ordinary life. A number of downsides made trying to recreate or deepen these experiences through continued drug use impractical. For some, further drug exploration often proved, over time, to be too taxing on their body. Others discovered they had no guarantee of what the next drug experience might be—transcendent or horrifying. There has never been a reliable means to control the experience. Others were eventually frustrated that they could sometimes access seemingly spiritual realms, but the insights did not seem to last. So, quite a few set out to India or other exotic places. They went in search of gurus who could show them how to access the spiritual realm and its true and lasting wisdom without using drugs.

high, but not free

One of my teachers, Ajahn Amaro, has offered us an analogy for how psychadelic drugs can affect our minds. If you want to clear up a plugged sink, he says, you can use a plunger or some Drano and, with some persistence and a little effort, you will ultimately get the dirt and hairballs out. Or you can take a sledgehammer and smash the whole sink open to get the hairballs out. Drugs are a bit like the sledgehammer. If you want to open your mind, you can do so slowly with meditation, study, and practice. Or you can blow your mind, full blast. It is up to you. You may have to pick up the pieces and glue them back together in order to wash dishes again.

Most spiritual seekers who have used drugs had similar experiences. They discovered that drugs could give them a glimpse of something extraordinary, but once the drugs stop working, they were back where they started. Personal transformation requires work, and most people will not find it in a pill or tab. Waking up is a lifetime proposal. Waking up takes (and actually *develops*) persistence, effort, acceptance—all wonderful spiritual qualities. Waking up is joyful work. A daily spiritual practice deepens our wisdom, understanding, ability to connect, and to have compassion and empathy for others. Real spiritual practice is a way of life, and for many, meditation experiences will result in depths of understanding far greater than any ever attained through drug use.

The more we open to our spiritual life, the more we see how valuable our mind and body are. We want to protect and take care of them. They are the means by which we wake up. They *are* what wakes up.

Kate, who is twenty now, learned the beauty of letting go of drug addiction and waking up to her life:

My freshman year of college was one of the hardest times in my life. Everything looked bleak to me, and I had endless questions about my self-worth and what to do with my life. On top of all of this, I had developed quite a pot habit. Once I even found myself driving an hour and back in a blizzard just to get to my friends, their music, and that perpetually packed bowl. I was using this drug to numb my mind and to forget my unanswered questions. I know this sounds like a huge cliché, but this is my actual experience of it.

Eventually I decided that I had an unhealthy psychologi-

cal addiction to pot and that I had to stop. Sometime in the spring, my parents suggested that I attend a meditation retreat. What I found was something that is virtually impossible to explain. I found the ability to know and love myself. I realized that what I would be doing in ten years was totally unimportant, and that being happy with what I was doing now was infinitely more important. The retreat gave me not only the ability to quit smoking pot, but the ability to appreciate that my mind is an amazing thing, and clogging it up is really rather boring and useless—a much less pure or interesting experience of the world.

Drug use can be a doorway that gives a small taste of our potential, of our creative or visionary nature, or of the spiritual realm, but ultimately, drugs are limited in their potential for awakening. As the saying goes: "Drugs can get us high but they cannot get us free." True freedom is not dependent on the use of a substance.

Finally, the proof is in the results. Most of us know friends or classmates who have taken drugs and had profound experiences, but when they returned to normal consciousness they could barely remember any details of their experience. They weren't changed in any lasting way, and the drug experience is just a vague memory. The proof of real change is in how we live our lives.

exercise in clarity

✳ During the course of a week, pay attention to how "non-drug intoxicants" affect you. What is your mind like after playing video games for hours, excessive TV watching, or listening to violent music? Do you feel present, joyful, connected to others? Or do you feel spaced out, isolated, aversive?

✳ If you feel drawn to stopping drug use (and are not currently under treatment for abuse or struggling with a drug addiction), make a commitment not to use any drugs or alcohol for one month and observe what happens. Write your reasons for stopping below, and refer back to them each time you feel drawn to use drugs. At the end of one month, evaluate and record what were the benefits and drawbacks.

part five

out in the world

seventeen

walking down the path
with others

Not associating with fools, but associating with the
wise, and honoring those who deserve honor—this
is supreme good fortune.

—Sutta Nipata 259

The monk Ananda, the Buddha's cousin, right-hand man,
and number-one attendant, was often the straight man
for the Buddha. The Buddha frequently corrected his innocent mistakes. One day after contemplating the community
of monks who supported his own practice, Ananda rushed to
the Buddha with his great discovery:

"Venerable Sir, this is half of the holy life, that is, good
friendship, good companionship, good comradeship."

"Not so, Ananda!"

Ananda looked surprised. He thought he had that one figured
out.

The Buddha continued, "This is the *entire* holy life. When a
monk has a good friend, a good companion, a good comrade. It
is expected that he will develop and cultivate the Noble Eightfold Path."

* * *

The teaching of this story is interpreted to mean that if we want to develop on our path, we need a wise friend, specifically the Buddha himself, or another enlightened or noble being. However, the Buddha has been dead for a long time now. If we can't be friends with him, what are the Buddha's teachings then on everyday friendships? And what might a spiritual friend look like?

choose our friendships wisely

In general, the Buddha emphasized that whom we choose to be friends with is very important. This is fairly obvious because who we spend time with affects us. We know this from our own experience, as Lia, who is sixteen, found:

> I was hanging out with a group of kids who were into smoking pot and skipping classes. I didn't really want to do that, but since my friends were, I started doing it too.

We are all susceptible to our environment. *Who* we spend time with (friends, parents, teachers), and *what* we spend time with (hanging out, watching TV, sitting in front of a computer, or playing music) affects our minds and sometimes our bodies. They influence what we think, say, and care about, and may shape our values and attitudes about life. Because at least to some degree we all can be influenced, the Buddha strongly suggested that we choose to hang out with wise friends who support us on our spiritual path.

company of the wise

The Buddha encouraged us to spend time with people who are wise, blameless, and skillful—people who act in ways that are non-harming. He mentioned four characteristics of wise friends.

1. helpful: someone who looks after you and your possessions, and helps you when you are fearful

2. trustworthy: someone who tells you his or her secrets, keeps your secrets, and doesn't let you down

3. intelligent: someone who points out what is good for you, prevents you from doing stupid things and supports you in making intelligent choices

4. sympathetic: someone who understands your problems, rejoices in your good luck, and stops people from speaking badly of you

Wise friends, in general, might be good listeners, or be impeccably honest. They might be kind to animals and encourage us to be, too. They might have a great relationship with their mom and help us with our problems with our mom. They might love to do service work and invite us along when they cook dinner at the soup kitchen. The Buddha would praise these kinds of friends. They live with integrity, and bring forth these qualities in us. They encourage us to be fully ourselves, and we like being around them because we trust them. Sometimes we even act a little smarter than we would have on our own, as fifteen-year-old Elise discovered:

> When I'm with my best friend I can talk about my problems in a way that I can't with anyone else. She really knows how to listen. Sometimes I feel like I get a new angle on the topics, not because she tells me what to do, but because I get understandings about myself more or say things in new ways, just because she is willing to listen, let me talk about exactly what's in my head, and she asks good questions.

company of fools

The Buddha also warned against the opposite: unwise companionship. He said we need to be careful not to associate with "fools" who are unwise, blameworthy, and unskillful. Sometimes we think of a fool as someone who makes us laugh, but in Buddhist terms, a fool is a person who is untrustworthy, has little integrity, and influences us in harmful ways. If we hang out with them, we become a fool too! The Buddha also mentioned four kinds of foolish friends.

1. self-serving: someone who takes advantage of you, acts out of fear, and tries to get what he or she wants out of you

2. "empty-mouthed": someone who speaks of things he or she plans to do to help you in the future but never does them; someone who mouths empty phrases

3. hypocritical: someone who praises you to your face but talks about you behind your back

4. bad influence: someone who encourages you to do things that may get you into trouble like drugs, alcohol, shoplifting

Fools are people whose behavior is easily disapproved of by those we trust. Such people might regularly talk badly of others, which could get on our nerves. We might have an intuitive sense that they are untrustworthy or telling us one thing but are acting in another way. They might encourage us to start smoking or doing drugs, or take up other harmful behaviors when we really don't want to. We might have fun with this person, but later on we think, "Man, I wish I'd never done that." Li, who is fifteen, discovered this the hard way:

When Susan started shoplifting we all thought she was crazy. I mean, her parents had money, why did she need to do that? But then Denise wanted Susan to like her, so she took a purse from a used clothing store. They said it was easy and fun and sort of dared me to do it. I didn't want them to stop liking me, so I stole some makeup. Sure I feel bad, but now I don't really have a choice if I want to stay friends with them.

Most important, when I am with these friends do I get to be me? Fourteen-year-old Jim was concerned with this question:

I have a lot of different groups of friends. One group is kind of weird because when I am with them I feel like I have to pretend to be somebody I'm not. I don't know why I hang out with them, I just do, even though I don't really like it.

hard choices

If we take an honest look at the friendships we presently have, based on the Buddhist criteria, a number of our friends may fall into the category of fools. So what do we do? Sometimes we have to make hard choices.

Marina, who is sixteen, told me that last year she reevaluated the people in her life. Some were old friends she didn't have a lot in common with any more. They were partiers but she, however, had begun intensive training in martial arts. She didn't want to stay up late drinking because she couldn't train well the next day. Hanging out with them felt strained, yet she had been friends with them for so long and couldn't imagine *not* being friends. But a part of her knew she had no choice. So she stopped hanging out with them. At first she struggled because they spread rumors about her, that she thought she was too good for them. But after a while they left her alone and she began to meet other kids with similar interests and felt more at home. She has since told me it was one of the best decisions she made with her life.

isolation

Many teens feel isolated in middle school or high school. Sometimes this isolation is chosen and sometimes it is imposed. Often because of their insecurities, some will ostracize others if they look different or don't fit in. This happened to fourteen-year-old Sandra:

> *I wore a radical outfit to school one day—I mean it wasn't anything that weird, but it was different than the other kids, and ever since then I have been considered the second most unpopular kid in the whole school. I hang my costume on a hook on my door to remind me of that day and how everything changed.*

When no one around us fits our criteria for "wise companionship," choosing isolation may be the highest wisdom. The Buddha said, "If you do not have a wise companion, solitude is best." Some young people I know honestly prefer their own company to that of the other kids in their school.

But sometimes we are isolated and want it to be different. If solitude is not a state that feels comfortable to us, what can we do to connect with good companions?

First of all, it is helpful to remember that high school is a time of rapid changes. Our friends today may not be our friends tomorrow. Popularity (the whole game of who's in who's out) changes as often as our clothing styles. The Buddhist teachings remind us not to take all this change personally, but that is easier said than done, of course!

If we desire wise friends, it is up to us to make an effort to find them. It may mean joining a club we never would have

wide awake

thought of joining before. It may also mean taking some risks. Is there one person in school who seems interesting and wise? Could we muster the courage to make the first move, to actually pursue a friendship, perhaps invite them for pizza with us after classes?

In order to find a wise friend, one must also undertake to be a wise friend. Each of us can actively work to embody the qualities of a wise friend, and to present ourselves to the world as someone worth getting to know.

When we hold an intention to bring high quality people into our lives, and when we start to be one ourselves, sometimes they come out of the woodwork. Be willing to be surprised. We may attract someone we never would have expected—a teacher, a next-door neighbor, even a grandparent.

they don't understand me anymore!

As we develop our spiritual lives, our friendships can get more complicated. Commonly, when we begin a meditation practice, we may fear that our friends will think we are weird or won't understand what we are doing.

When I came back from Asia after I started practicing meditation, I was scared to tell my friends. I thought for sure they would think I was a freak, since nobody I knew in America meditated. In my mind, I created fantasies about how I would be ostracized, and in a knee-jerk way, I began to feel a little superior. "Well, they won't understand me, but that's okay because I've found the *Truth*." While my conceit helped me protect myself against the very real fear that I would be rejected, it actually made me feel more lonely since it disconnected me from everyone else. Eventually, I knew I had to tell my friends about my leap into Buddhism.

I remember sitting in Prospect Park in Brooklyn with my best friend, Darcy, who had spent the year studying to be an actress in New York the same year I was in Asia. I was terrified how she would react to my new spiritual life. I took a deep breath and said, "I have something important to tell you. I think I'm a Buddhist." "Wow," she said, "What does that mean?" So I explained to her how I had spent weeks in retreat meditating, where I had stripped away and examined everything I had identified as "me." I talked about the psychological insights I had uncovered—like, my self-esteem is dependent on people's attention—and about the peace of quieting my mind. I tried to make it sound as "normal" as possible, but I steeled myself against the potential upcoming scorn. As I held my breath she said to me, "My God, Diana, it sounds exactly like what we've been doing in acting school!" We both started laughing. I felt such a sense of relief.

I soon found that even if my friends weren't Buddhist, a lot of them practiced some of the principles of Buddhism, without the Buddhist lingo. Many of them were kind and compassionate. Some were wise or had high integrity. I had been so worried I wouldn't be able to relate to people because of my Buddhism, but the truth was, when I was fully myself and was tapped into what was good in everyone, we could easily be friends. It was understandable to me that my friends didn't necessarily want to talk about Buddhism, so I found other people with whom I could talk. I have heard one teacher say, a lot changes when we stop trying to be a "Buddhist"—meaning acting out of our ideas about what a Buddhist is—and start trying to be a "Buddha"—acting from our ordinary integrity and kindness.

In truth, I did let go of some friends. Some people *didn't* understand me and ultimately, over time, I stopped seeing these people. Sometimes I felt a sense of loss, and sometimes I simply accepted the inevitable. And slowly, more and more "spiritual friends" came into my life.

kalyana mitta—spiritual friendships

It almost goes without saying that the best kind of friend to have when we are on a spiritual path is a spiritual friend, someone who can support us and walk with us down the spiritual path. The Buddhist term *kalyana mitta* (kah-lee-AH-na-MEET-ah) is used to mean a spiritual friend who is a peer or supportive buddy throughout our spiritual journey. This friend helps us over the rough parts of the path, directs us when we have forgotten our inner compass, inspires us when we feel lost, and keep us laughing when we have lost our sense of humor. When we meet a true spiritual friend, we know deep inside that we have found a kind of soul mate, someone who accepts us as we are.

I have a friend named Amy whom I met in 1990 when I was on a three-month meditation retreat. She left chocolate kisses in my shoe. I am not sure how, but somehow she knew I loved chocolate. When we finally spoke to each other, we couldn't believe how much we had in common. We stayed up most of the night discussing the past three months—how we had conquered boredom and frustration and found clarity on the other side, mystical states of mind we had encountered, and the people we hadn't yet met, but with whom we had fallen in love, anyway. I could trust her completely. Over the years we have stayed friends, even though we have never lived near each other. We call each other for advice about relationships, work, and especially about the dharma. When we visit we talk until our mouths are sore about our spiritual practices. I remember once saying "Amy, I rely on you so much. I'm starting to feel guilty." "Diana," she said, "We're spiritual friends. You're not relying just on me, but relying on the dharma. And I rely on you, too." She is my true "dharma sister."

sangha—creating community

I have discovered that the more I have emphasized my spiritual growth, meditation, and precepts practice, the more I have drawn people to me who were also seekers on a spiritual path. Whenever I went on retreats, I made a point to talk with people with whom I seemed to have a connection, especially younger practitioners. Then I worked hard to stay in touch with them, or if they lived near me, to spend time with them. Now I have lots of friends who are also on the dharma path and I feel grateful for that.

Eventually, as we commit more and more to our spiritual life, our group of spiritual friends increases. We develop what is called *Sangha*—the community of spiritual practitioners who support each other in holding forth to our heart's deepest intent. Traditionally, this word refers to the community of monks and nuns around the Buddha or in a monastery. These were the Noble Sangha, people who followed the Eightfold Path to develop virtues like morality, kindness, and renunciation. That sangha exists all over Asia today and in some places in the west. But these days in America, we also use the word sangha to mean our own group of spiritual friends, or a community or group who practice together. One does not have to be a monk or nun to be called sangha.

Matt started meditating when he was eighteen, but spent years feeling lonely in his spiritual life. He was younger than most of the people he met on retreats, so he kept to himself because he couldn't relate to people in their forties and fifties. One day he decided to change the situation. He started an email list for young people who meditate in the San Francisco Bay Area, where he lives. Soon lots of people joined and after a while they were having potlucks, dances, and parties. Eventually, seventy people joined the list and he had all sorts of new friends who shared similar interests. Matt felt such a sense of happiness in creating this community and being able to extend it to others.

wide awake

When I think about the things I am most grateful for in my life, my friendships are at the top of the list. When I think about what gives me the most joy in my life, again, I think of my friends (right up there with the dharma!). Friendships are a such an integral part of our lives—a part we can develop, explore, practice with, and learn from. As the Buddha urged us to acknowledge, wise friendships can be all of the spiritual life.

exercise your relationships

Reflect on these questions:

* Who are your closest friends?

* What group do you hang out with?

* What kind of effect do they have on you?

* If you could make one change in your friendships, what would it be?

eighteen

what comes next?
finding right livelihood

The creatures that inhabit this earth—be they human
beings or animals—are here to contribute, each in
its own particular way, to the beauty and prosperity
of the world.

—His Holiness the Fourteenth Dalai Lama

When I finished college I felt like my life was over.

Ironically, the year before it seemed like I was on top. I knew all the right people, belonged to the right clubs, and knew how to ace exams. People respected me. I coasted through my senior year because I knew the system so well.

But when I graduated, I was thrown out into the "real" world where nobody knew me. I hadn't made any career plans. I had spent so much time in high school and college doing what everybody else wanted for me that I had no idea what *I* wanted for me.

I knew how to navigate classrooms, homework, teachers, and grades. However, I had never taken a class on how to live my life. No teacher showed me how to pay bills or rent an apartment, or cook a meal. How strange that we devote twenty-one years of our lives to studying topics that won't do us much good in the next fifty years! Sure, I could write a passable History paper. So what?

Some of us may now be dealing with questions of where to

go next. This uncertainty, exciting as can be, forces us to be the decision maker of our lives. If we don't go on to college, these struggles hit us right after high school, or even earlier if we drop out or take time off. Of course, some may have to find a job right away to support themselves or their family. Others may still be in school thinking, the real world is coming, what will I do? Still others are already sure what they want to do, but are wondering how their chosen work might fit into a Buddhist framework.

This chapter brings Buddhist wisdom to the thorny issue of what comes next. In particular, we will explore the challenge of choosing a livelihood that will be both satisfying and of benefit to the world.

right livelihood

In Chapter 4, we talked about the Four Noble Truths. The fourth truth, as you recall, is called the Eightfold Path, or, the way out of suffering. The Eightfold Path teaches how to live a spiritual life in harmony with others and in keeping with the teachings of the Buddha. One part of the Eightfold Path is called Right Livelihood. When we consider finding our place in the world, the guidelines for Right Livelihood are an excellent starting point.

"Livelihood" means how we make money and survive in the world, through job or career. "Right," in Buddhist terms, means that which leads to true happiness and doesn't cause suffering to ourselves or others. So, Right Livelihood is the Buddha's recommendations on working in the world in a way that brings happiness. Right Livelihood is just as important to the whole of the Eightfold Path as meditation is. So even if we have meditated for twenty years, if we are a petty thief, then we are not leading a truly spiritual life.

At the time of the Buddha, many people left worldly pursuits and became monks and nuns. The Buddha considered monasticism to be the ultimate career path because following the Buddha's teaching is easier in a monastery, where everyone else is practicing in the same way we are. Practicing his teachings when we live unsupported out in the world requires a special kind of determination.

I don't imagine many of you are planning to shave your head, give up your worldly possessions, and join a monastery. And historically, neither did all of the Buddha's followers choose the monastic life. The Buddha appreciated the commitment of these lay people, and provided them with guidelines for living and working in the world. He asked lay people to acquire enough wealth to support their family, to save for hard times, and to give away excess to the poor. He encouraged lay people to take care of their parents in their old age, to provide for their children until they were self-sufficient, and to live a blameless life, meaning one that followed the Five Precepts: not to kill, steal, harm through sexuality, lie, or misuse intoxicants.

Determining our livelihood is extremely important, of course, because most people spend the majority of their waking hours engaged in their work life. The Buddha suggested that making a living in a way that broke any of the Five Precepts was not Right Livelihood. If this seems dogmatic, then we are missing the point. What the Buddha meant was that it is up to us to explore how our work either prevents or creates harmony in ourselves and the world.

The Buddha believed that having a job that involved killing would break the first precept and cause harm. He would strongly oppose a career path as a hit man or woman. But other kinds of killing also are discouraged. The Buddha was concerned with the welfare of all creatures, including animals. Any job that killed animals (such as a butcher or exterminator) was not considered right livelihood. Selling guns or other weapons is also discouraged. He also prohibited jobs that manufactured or sold poisons. You may question whether any profession that involves potential killing, even if the killing is indirect, is breaking the precept. How about a noncombatant soldier? What if you worked as a scientist who developed nuclear weapons? What if the company you work for dumps toxic chemicals into a living waterway?

The second precept of not stealing would be broken if you decided your lifelong ambition was to hold up the local 7-Eleven, or any profession based on stealing. Some livelihoods you could choose break the second precept in obvious ways, but you might ask yourself, what about working for corporations that makes clothing overseas and pay the workers next to nothing? Is this stealing? What about wage inequity—when a CEO of a company makes thousands of dollars more than a worker. Is that stealing? Recently, in the news there have been instances of high level executives directly stealing from their corporations, or "padding the books" in their favor. Of course this is breaking the second precept and is not recommended for a livelihood choice, although an ethical CEO is most welcome.

Breaking the third precept of sexual misconduct might be the livelihood of working in the pornography industry or in a business that sexually exploits women, men, or children. What about working in advertising, where sexuality is often misused to sell everything from cars to shampoo? And if you decide that selling with sex falls outside right livelihood, is the whole music industry off limits? These kinds of questions make our livelihood decisions less black and white, and more interesting.

Working in a business that required you to lie would break the fourth precept. Of course, when you start a job, you don't always know whether you will be asked to lie or falsify information in some way. If your job does not usually entail lying, but you are asked to not disclose something potentially damaging to your employer, would you have to quit? How would the Buddha have felt about a career as a journalist for a news source that manufactures stories for the public? How about lying to get a job in the first place?

Finally, any job that involved the selling or use of drugs or alcohol would break the fifth precept against intoxicants. Owning a liquor store, dealing drugs, selling marijuana, and running drugs would not be considered right livelihood. Would working as a bartender, as harmless as it seems, break the precept?

It is unrealistic to think that any job will be perfectly pure, so when making decisions or checking out what you are drawn to, you can start by eliminating the obvious violations of the precepts and then make your own decisions about what feels comfortable. It is wise to research the ethical values of any company or organization you plan to work for, although unfortunately you may not find much available information. What if all corporations were required to take and publish an ethical inventory?

We have looked closely at what Right Livelihood is not. What about what it is? Well, Right Livelihood can be fulfilled in a variety of ways. One could be an artist, musician, craftsperson, house builder, social worker, doctor, metal worker, teacher, nonprofit organizer, activist, writer, factory-worker, clown . . .

Each of us has particular talents, skills, and preferences that we would like to see manifested in our work in the world. We might have loved computers since we were younger and plan to

in choosing right livelihood, consider the five precepts

1. Not killing/harming
2. Not stealing
3. Not harming with sexuality
4. Not lying
5. Not misusing intoxicants

become a programmer. We may know we want to be a dancer, or have always dreamed about playing guitar in a rock band. How does your particular interest and dream measure up to this description of Right Livelihood? Of course, the Buddha cannot tell you what to do. If you have always wanted to be a soldier, don't let these guidelines stop you, but please choose your job consciously. The five precepts are a good framework for making us more aware of the consequences of our actions.

Right Livelihood is any job to which we feel drawn that first, does not cause harm to others, and second, lets us fully express ourselves, our talents and our gifts. Because Right Livelihood is grounded in the awareness of interconnection—that our actions affect each other—following Right Livelihood will serve others in the end. Each of us, fully being ourselves in the world, sharing our gifts and talents, has a transformative quality. When you meet a person who is doing work that she loves and is clearly beneficial to others, you can palpably feel something special about the person. She almost glows with drive and mission. Others around her become inspired to do the work that fulfills each of them.

how do i choose?

But what if making a decision about our future is not easy? Many of my teenage friends get unusually quiet when asked the perennial adult question: What are you going to do with your life?

Of course, some teens have no choice, the family has a career path that all the kids are expected to follow, like with Susan, who is fourteen:

My family is all career navy, so I just assume that's what I'll do. At least that's what my parents are expecting of me.

Or others, like seventeen-year-old Mark, know we will do whatever we can to help our family make ends meet:

*I knew that when I finished high school I would have to find a
job right away, probably at the factory in town because my
mother had no money to send me to college.*

Some of us suffer from having too many options. Those who
grew up middle-class or above may have been given the incredible gift to not to have to worry so much about money. When
making money is not the top priority, they could become anything. But sometimes this freedom doesn't feel like a blessing.
One of my friends is so upset by the seemingly limitless possibilities that she feels paralyzed:

*I'm good at a lot of things and I like so many that I don't know
what to do. When I look out at the world with the overwhelming choices I seriously want to give up. How will I ever decide? I have been depressed for the last year because of this.*

Others—especially those who grew up without a lot of privilege—also are daunted by the task of creating a future. They may
wonder if they will ever get a break. Thinking about the future can
be like a scary black hole. The world seems overwhelming; the
classified ads, with their tiny type, lists hundreds of opportunities
that we may not even know if we are either interested in or qualified for. Living is expensive. Can one ever find the right next step?

Parental pressures don't make decisions any easier. Alex,
who is fifteen and thinking about his career, told me:

*My dad's a doctor, so of course he wants me to be a doctor.
But I think I would make a terrible doctor, as I get sick at the
sight of blood. But how can I tell him? It will break his heart.*

Parental expectations are extremely common, and usually their
expectations are not without reason. Our parents love us and
want us to have a good life. Some are worried about money and

wide awake ·

246

try to imagine lucrative careers so that we will not have financial
worries. Or they want us to be what they never had a chance to
be, or allowed themselves to be. Some parents can't understand
why what would make *them* happy would not also make their
child very happy. Jade, who is eighteen, dealt with this problem:

> My mother always wanted to be an actress, but she never
> made it. So she started taking me out on auditions for kids'
> TV shows and commercials from when I was little. I didn't
> even like acting, but she was so insistent. When I got older I
> began to rebel by doing lots of drugs and gaining weight so
> no one would pick me for parts.

A balanced position for us to take would be to neither reject outright our parents desires for us, nor to accept without question.
Parents have good intentions in their wishes for us, and we
should learn what those are. We need to try to separate their
wisdom from their fears, which may be tangled in there, too—
this can take a lot of patient conversation. When talking to our
parents about life plans that are different than their wishes for
us, clear communication is key. It can be helpful to find supportive allies adults can trust, who can explain our point of view in a
way our parents can understand.

steps on the path

But how can we choose what to do with our lives, and what if
we choose the *wrong* thing? I used to worry about that. It was one
of the scariest questions in my life right after high school. I felt
paralyzed to choose. I remember taking long walks in the woods
with my dad and crying. I was so worried that if I took a step toward one kind of career path, I would lose an opportunity to do
something else. And that might have been the *right* thing, and
then I would have blown it.

My dad listened carefully. Then he told me to relax. He reminded me not to be afraid to make mistakes. "Of course you'll make mistakes," he said. "The only way you will know if you want to be something is if you try. It's a process of elimination. I went half way through law school and discovered I didn't want to be a lawyer. So I took off and traveled around the country for a year. Later I realized I wanted to go into the business world. Try a path and find out. That's how you discover what you love to do." My father's words gave me the confidence to apply for my first job—as a stage manager for a play.

The surest way to determine whether we are on the right track is to take a step on the path. Try something and see what happens. If we want to be a trapeze artist, we might find someone to apprentice with. We can give it a try, and then discover we are afraid of heights. But we still wildly love the circus, so we begin training as a bareback rider, and discover, while we are not a talented gymnast, we have a talent for taming horses. We will only know the truth for ourselves if we try. What we do at one point in our life may not be what we do forever. Statistics say the average person makes a career change seven times in his or her life. One friend of mine has been a bricklayer, a chef, a painter, a mom, a psychic, a teacher, and a hot air balloonist.

Since the time that I cried with my dad, I have had a lot of different jobs in my life. I have waitressed at a sushi bar, telemarketed children's books, sold clothing from Bali, babysat, taught school, written for magazines, organized conferences, and canvassed door to door to stop pollution.

I tried all these jobs and each one led me closer to where I am now—a Buddhist writer, teacher, and activist. I got where I am by pursuing the things I loved the most. I trusted that my interest in meditation, young people and politics would lead to something. And it did. Many years later, I took a job with the Buddhist Peace Fellowship, where I was able to bring my Buddhism to working for social change, and to teaching meditation to young

wide awake .

people around the world. This synthesis will be the subject of the next chapter. I love my work, but it took me a long time to find it. I didn't start out knowing immediately what I wanted to do.

One of my heroines, Beatrice Wood, who incidentally lived to be over one hundred, was considered a living national treasure for the craftsmanship of her ceramics—bawdy, sexy clay sculptures. She didn't start this career until she was in her forties.

My dad helped me see that if I step on the path and it is "wrong" I am going to find that out sooner or later, and so will you. Should the first path you try prove disappointing, take what you have learned and use that to make a decision for your next step, perhaps down an entirely different road. And, yes, by choosing one job, you will be shutting some doors but you also will be opening up others.

how we do it counts

Ultimately, it may not matter what work we do, but the manner in which we do the work. Some jobs provide more opportunity for growth and understanding, and others may be repetitive, boring or unchallenging. However, if we can approach our work, whether it is an afterschool job or the start of the career of our dreams, with some of the principles we have been exploring throughout this book, we will be in good stead.

We can bring awareness into even the most tedious of jobs. Any work we do can be an opportunity for waking up, just by remembering to bring ourselves into the present moment. We can bring loving-kindness and compassion to our co-workers or to customers at the pizza joint. We can practice not judging ourselves or others. We can notice equanimity in our mind and cultivate more of it through taking the difficulties of our job more lightly. We can stay true to our integrity, even when it is challenged. Work is a wonderful opportunity to practice the dharma!

Twenty years ago, if you asked young people whom they admired, they gave the names of heroic men and women throughout history such as Abraham Lincoln, Mother Teresa, Martin Luther King, Jr., Gandhi, or Amelia Earhart.

A recent survey concluded that teens' heroes these days are mostly celebrities like Britney Spears, Leonardo Di Caprio, Winona Ryder, and Shaq. In the United States, we live in a culture that deifies stars. They are the heroes of our times. They are not famous for their wisdom, compassion, or acts of extraordinary generosity. They are famous for being highly visible in movies or making hit recordings, or scoring thirty points a game.

Who we look up to can have a huge effect on what we do with our lives. We want to be like our heroes. Unfortunately, if our heroes are not people who live a blameless life (aligned with the five precepts) and we choose to be like them, we may emulate them to negative consequences. We may think pursuing money or fame will give us happiness. We may also wind up feeling that our own lives pale in comparison. Can you find others to model your life on who inspire you in a different way? A hero doesn't have to be someone famous. Even your neighbor or your aunt could be your hero.

My friend James tells a story about a nearby tollbooth that he loves. Whenever he drives up to it, he keeps his fingers crossed, hoping he will get to hand his money to a particular tollbooth guy. This one man is his favorite because the man takes the money with incredible care and attentiveness. James says that it feels like he is being blessed by the man. Doing nothing more than collecting a toll can become an act of grace.

The Buddha suggested that as we enter the world of work and career, we make sure our desires follow the Five Precepts, so that we don't harm ourselves or others through our livelihood. Then, as we explore our possibilities, we need to trust our inner unfolding. Each of us has an expression of who we are that is waiting to come into the world. If we are diligent and attentive, if we learn to look deeply into our hearts, the gift will flower. When we allow who we are to blossom, the world will benefit. And we will have found Right Livelihood. Pioneer of modern dance Martha Graham said it best:

> *There is a vitality, a life force, a quickening that is translated through you into action, and because there is only one of you in all time, this expression is unique. And if you block it, it will never exist through any other medium, and be lost. The world will not have it. It is not your business to determine how good it is, nor how it compares with other expressions. It is your business to keep it yours, clearly and directly, to keep the channel open.*

exercise your future

Reflect on the following questions:

✷ What messages have you received from your parents about your career path?

✷ What are your fears about entering the working world?

✳ Who are your heroes? What are these people's lives like, and why do you like them? Are their lives good examples of Right Livelihood?

✳ What do you think you have to offer the world? What is your special gift for humanity?

nineteen

don't just sit there, do something!: socially engaged buddhism

It is my experience that the world itself has a role to play in our liberation. Its very pressures, pains, and risks can wake us up—release us from the bonds of ego and guide us home to our vast true nature.

—Joanna Macy, American Buddhist teacher

Could we exclude anyone from our compassion any more than the sun could exclude any from the warmth and radiance of its rays?

—Chagdad Tulku Rinpoche, Tibetan Buddhist teacher

We live in challenging times. Scan the newspapers for the word on the latest wars, deaths, and violence. The week I wrote this, three hundred people died in Somalia from war. Suicide bombers and the military response thwart any possibility of peace in the Middle East. The ozone layer is deteriorating; the oceans are so polluted now that there is an advisory against eating some kinds of fish. In the United States, gang members killed four innocent people in a drive-by shooting. A five-year-old child shot another five-year-old. What a crazy world!

A common stereotype suggests that in the midst of this worldly suffering, most Buddhists sit on their cushions staring at their navel all day. Is it that Buddhists don't see that the world is a mess? Do they not know that people are dying from poverty, disease, and war, and that the environment is being destroyed? Does meditating make any difference in light of the suffering in the world?

These are the kinds of questions I had when I began my meditation practice. I had been an activist for most of my life. When I was thirteen, my mother took me to my first rally against nuclear weapons, which became the main focus of my activism from high school on. In college I joined a women's center and women's political action group. I even started a political theater company that brought creativity and humor—music and performance—to political rallies and demonstrations.

While in India, after college, I fell in love with Buddhism. I fantasized about meditating for the rest of my life. I imagined becoming a hermit in a mountain cave, living off boiled nettles and practicing yoga and meditation for years on end.

For several years I put my activism on hold. I lived in meditation centers and pretended to stop caring about the world. I convinced myself that in order to practice the dharma I had to give up being an activist. Activists are loud, angry, and opinionated. Buddhists are peaceful, focused inward, and unattached. The world's problems simply don't affect Buddhists.

I held a silly notion of what being a Buddhist was (*and* what being an activist was!). I didn't believe that I could be both. But in separating one piece of myself from another piece, I felt fragmented. That split felt uncomfortable because deep inside I knew that, somehow, my Buddhist practice had to be connected to working for social change. I just wasn't sure how. Most of my teachers suggested I would be able to be both an activist and a Buddhist, but none of them gave me clear descriptions of what that would look like.

A few years later I met a wonderful teacher named Joanna

Macy, who is an activist, ecologist, and a Buddhist. She was also deeply concerned about nuclear weapons and she, along with others I soon read about, was developing and practicing this very combination: Buddhism and social change. The two fit together harmoniously. I knew I had found my home where the two sides of me could peacefully coexist, and even complement each other. I became a "socially engaged" Buddhist.

In 1995, I created the Buddhist Alliance for Social Engagement or BASE program for the Buddhist Peace Fellowship, a socially engaged Buddhist non-profit organization. Through BASE, groups of about ten people, of all different ages and backgrounds, spend six months volunteering or working in service and social change fields like hospices, homeless clinics, youth gardens, inner city schools, and environmental agencies. The members meet weekly to meditate, study, and talk about the intersection of Buddhism and social change. I loved creating this program as it brought together all of my interests. BASE has helped almost 200 people practice socially engaged Buddhism in different parts of the U.S. and Canada, and has offered thousands of volunteer hours to organizations and people in need.

This chapter will further explore socially engaged Buddhism, its roots and history. We will look at how we can bring engagement into our spiritual lives and find our place of service in the world. For inspiration I will introduce you to the extraordinary people who embody this ideal.

socially engaged buddhism

As witness to the French colonization of Vietnam and the subsequent Vietnam War, a young Vietnamese Buddhist monk named Thich Nhat Hanh (who I have spoken of throughout the book) was disturbed by the suffering of his people. Villages were being bombed, villagers were being raped and murdered. But he was a monk, and traditionally, monks are not supposed to be involved in politics of any sort. At first he was perplexed by the conflict between his desire to help, and the rules and assumptions of the established monastic tradition. Later he realized he could do both, and said,

> *When I was in Vietnam, so many of our villages were being bombed. Along with my monastic brothers and sisters, I had to decide what to do. Should we continue to practice in our monasteries, or should we leave the meditation halls in order to help the people who were suffering under the bombs? After careful reflection, we decided to do both—to go out and help people and to do so in mindfulness. We called it engaged Buddhism. Mindfulness must be engaged. Once there is seeing, there must be acting. Otherwise, what is the use of seeing?*

Thich Nhat Hanh, or Thay, as we call him (Thay means teacher in Vietnamese and is pronounced like TIE) and his friends responded to the war by helping villagers rebuild their homes after the bombings; caring for the sick, elderly, and orphaned; and by protesting the war. In 1965, he founded the School for Youth for Social Service, where young people trained to relieve the suffering caused by war and extend their compassionate action towards all Vietnamese, regardless of their political orientation. The school was founded on Buddhist ideals, and students practiced together in a community that provided spiritual support and inspiration. Thay and his students were also outspoken advocates of ending war. Thay refused to side with either North or South Vietnam. He stood only for peace. Thay was a contemporary model and inspiration for socially engaged Buddhism, and joins models throughout Buddhist history, like King Ashoka, the first Buddhist king.

Socially engaged Buddhism brings Buddhist teachings, practice and wisdom together with action for progressive social change. Through Buddhist practice we come to a greater under-standing of ourselves, and rather than denying the world, our wisdom helps us to be effective agents of change. We are work-ing to end suffering on all levels—personal, social, political, and ecological. In bringing their spiritual lives to their work, Bud-dhists have started hospice programs for the dying, job and liter-acy programs for the homeless or unemployed, and other outreach programs. Other Buddhist practitioners are activists who meditate in front of prisons during death penalty execu-

king ashoka

In 270 B.C., a King named Ashoka conquered half of the Indian subcontinent. He was a violent and barbaric man. One day, after winning a particularly bloody bat-tle, he saw hundreds of mutilated dead bodies strewn across the battlefield. As he surveyed the scene, a serene monk passed by him. It is said that in the mo-ment King Ashoka saw the monk, he knew he had made a huge mistake, and that instead of conquering the world, he needed to conquer his mind. He sought out Buddhist teachings, became a Buddhist, and then nonviolently converted most of India to Buddhism. He put the Buddhist teachings into practice by building hospitals, programs to alleviate poverty, stopping all wars and bringing peace to the land. Because he took the first Buddhist precept so seriously and particularly loved animals, he was the first person in recorded his-tory to build veterinary clinics for animals. He was one of the first socially engaged Buddhists in history.

tions or hold vigils to protest nuclear weapons. Still others have created Buddhist groups and educational programs to address issues like racism, sexism, and homophobia.

no separation, no enemy

For socially engaged Buddhists, personal and social change are not separate. Both are developed simultaneously. Our meditation practice develops our compassion, the wish for others to be free from suffering. Compassionate feelings often lead to a desire to act to help end others' suffering. Through acts of compassion, our wisdom grows—we see interconnections more clearly—and our meditation strengthens; as wisdom strengthens, more acts of compassion naturally flow. And the circle completes itself.

The Buddhist principle of interconnection reminds us how closely intertwined we are with all life on this planet. None of us exist in isolation. Having compassion for others is a natural response of an awakened heart, because all creatures are part of us. Compassion for others and compassion for self are two sides of the same coin of interdependence. Compassion is not pity. It does not mean we feel sorry for someone. Compassion is the true desire to alleviate suffering, frequently followed by acts to do so.

Simultaneously addressing the suffering in the world and working for personal transformation makes sense. If we meditate and work only on ourselves, we can become self-centered and escapist. If we work only on the world, we might become burned-out and angry. Instead, we can work on both. Seventeen-year-old Michael made this point:

> I can be really judgmental of myself because I notice a split between what I do and how I want the world to be. That's what I want to work on, like that Gandhi quote, "Embody the

alice project school

Valentino Giacomin was a school teacher in Italy, where he developed a program to bring Buddhist ethics, wisdom, and meditation teachings into the classroom. He decided to take his teaching methods to Sarnath, India, where the Buddha first taught.

On a dusty field, Valentino built a school with spacious open-air classrooms, and painted it different shades of blue. He planted exotic flowers and vegetable gardens all around the school. Then he invited in the local children, many of whom were extremely poor. He taught these children reading and writing and traditional school subjects, along with Buddhist values of kindness, compassion and awareness. He did not try to convert them to Buddhism, but taught tolerance and respect for all religions. He called the school Awakening Special Education-Alice Project.

Slowly the children were transformed. These low caste, poor children did better on school and psychological tests than any other children in their area. As they learned to read and write, they developed self-esteem. Soon the children's villages were affected too. Valentino assisted the families in getting medical attention and helped them to develop small businesses. Later the parents came to the night school, and they learned to read as well. Over three hundred children now attend the school. It is an extraordinary example of socially engaged Buddhism.

change you seek in the world." I have all these ideas about changing the world and they sound nice, but they don't matter if I can't go to school without getting completely irritated by half the student body.

Since meditating, I have begun to have more compassion for people who have a different idea than I do. I can have an understanding of them, not hatred or animosity. Recently I saw a bumper sticker that said, "Mean people are suffering." That seems to sum it all up. I can develop compassion for myself, and also for my so-called "enemies." I try not to hold my anger. Even if I am battling with people I disagree fiercely with, I don't hate them or force them out of my heart. And of course that improves my meditation practice.

Like Michael, who discovered his compassion through meditation, Buddhist practice can bring us to this place in our hearts where we find we do not even hate our enemies. No greater story illustrates this than that of the Dalai Lama of Tibet.

In 1957, the Chinese army invaded the Buddhist country of Tibet, which lies across China's western border and is about one-seventeenth the size of the U.S. The army destroyed the Tibetan Buddhist temples, murdered one million people and imprisoned many thousand others, and sent hundreds of thousands of Tibetans into exile. His Holiness the Dalai Lama who is both the spiritual and political leader of Tibet, was a young man of nineteen at the time of the invasion. In 1959, he and his family escaped Tibet in a treacherous journey across the snowy mountains to Dharamsala, India, where he lives today. He has never returned to his homeland.

In spite of the continued genocide of the Tibetan people, loss of the Tibetan culture and religion, and the loss of his country, His Holiness (as we call him) appears to me to be one of the kindest and most compassionate people I have ever met. He says that because of his spiritual practice, he does not hate the Chinese. Instead he has tremendous compassion for them because he understands the teachings of karma—violent actions lead to unhappy results.

His Holiness has said,

> *The problems we face today—violent conflicts, destruction of nature, poverty, hunger, and so on—are mainly problems created by humans. They can be resolved, but only through human effort, understanding and the development of a sense of brotherhood and sisterhood. To do this we need to develop a universal responsibility for one another and for the planet we share, based on a good heart and awareness.*

Equipped with this extraordinary courage and kindness, he works tirelessly for a free homeland, yet he appears to be unattached to his goal.

cultivating our minds

One common belief is that we are born a certain way and we are stuck with those qualities. Either you are born to be Mother Teresa or you are ordinary, like everyone else. But according to the teachings of the Buddha, this understanding is not quite right. Through practice we can develop qualities of kindness, compassion, and generosity. We can develop equanimity, patience, determination and nonattachment to help us with the courageous task of serving the world.

Any of us can cultivate beautiful qualities through spiritual practice. My friend Tempel, who you may recall from Chapter 11, received *metta* (loving-kindness) from his dog, practiced *metta* meditation on a three-month retreat. He spent up to sixteen hours each day generating the wish that all beings would be happy and sending metta to all beings. When he returned home from the retreat, at first he felt loving toward everyone, even his friend with whom he usually fought. Slowly his normal (often aversion-filled) mind came back until he felt as if he had never done the long retreat. How depressing!

Previously he had been working at a shelter for homeless teens, many of whom were in and out of juvenile hall. The teens often made fun of his meditation practice, and of him because they thought he wasn't tough. They joked a lot at his expense and often angered him. Because he felt judged, he found himself to be quite uptight around these teens.

After the retreat he went back to the shelter and just when he was considering that he might have to quit his job, out of the blue, the metta kicked in in his mind. He kept wishing everyone would be happy, including the kid who made fun of the way he shot a basket. He found himself sending metta to the teens, the staff, and even his boss, with whom he didn't particularly get along. He realized that although the metta wasn't right there on the surface, when he was in a difficult situation, the metta came out unbidden. It felt like a miracle. Tempel experienced deep gratitude for all the meditation practice he did, that allowed his mind of metta to come to the rescue when it was most needed and could most benefit others. And because he was so laid back and loving thanks to the metta, the teens responded to him and began to listen to and respect him.

being a bodhisattva

In Buddhism there is the idea of the awakened being, or Bodhisattva. The terms come from two Sanskrit words—*Bodhi* meaning awake, and *sattva* meaning being. Bodhisattvas are beings who become enlightened for the sake of all beings. They practice to end suffering for everyone. The Bodhisattva vow taken by practitioners in the Zen tradition goes:

wide awake ·

Beings are numberless, I vow to save them.
Delusions are inexhaustible, I vow to end them.
Dharma gates are boundless, I vow to enter them.
Buddha's way is unsurpassable, I vow to become it.

Throughout Buddhist texts and legends, a Bodhisattva is portrayed as an exalted being with magical powers and great compassion who helps the world. Kwan Yin is a famous Bodhisattva in Buddhist mythology whose name means "one who hears the cries of the world." Throughout China and Japan, her compassion and strength is called upon in times of need. Another Bodhisattva, Manjushri, is depicted with a "sword of wisdom" that can cut through any confusion.

A socially engaged interpretation of the Bodhisattva is called the Ordinary Bodhisattva. Ordinary Bodhisattvas are not exalted beings, they don't have to be anyone special or supernatural. Instead, anyone can become an Ordinary Bodhisattva, a person who chooses to act with as much wisdom and compassion as they possibly can for the sake of the world. This kind of Bodhisattva is dedicated to the ending of all forms of suffering—personal of course, but also social, political, and ecological—and will devote his or her life to seeing this realized.

The Ordinary Bodhisattva cares deeply about the world, wants to work for its healing, and wants to grow spiritually in the process. They develop Bodhisattva qualities like compassion and sincerity over a lifetime. It is a long process! They don't have to be a great world leader, only someone who cares and chooses to act for others. They might be an artist or a comedian or a doctor, or maybe they tutor children in math on Thursdays. They are on the path toward greater compassion and wisdom for the sake of all beings.

how can we help?

How can any of us work towards becoming an Ordinary Bodhisattva? How can we get involved in service or social change? Many teens have told me that they have been meaning to volunteer or be politically active, but haven't quite known how to begin. The suffering in the world can feel overwhelming, and there seems to be enough work for many lifetimes. We may feel confused, unsure of the best and most effective way to get involved. We can even feel paralyzed and do nothing, if it seems that in choosing one task, another equally important one might be undone. Where can we best use our talents? How will we know where to step in?

The rule of thumb is to go where our heart is drawn.

When I was in Sri Lanka I met a Dutch woman named Sophie who was working at an orphanage. She got up every morning at six A.M. and for eight hours played with and tended to newborn babies. Astonishingly, she never seemed to get tired of it. I started to feel guilty when I compared myself to her. I didn't feel like I could ever have her enthusiasm. I once had worked at an orphanage in Calcutta, and I had been bored to death. I felt I had failed at service.

One day we went to the beach together, and when were floating on our backs in the cool blue water, I finally said, "Sophie, you are so much kinder than I am. You are so good at working with the children. I feel incompetent compared to you."

Sophie turned to me and said, "I *love* it! I work there everyday because it makes me happy. You have different skills. You are a good organizer and writer. You teach meditation. I could never do those things. Diana, the best change happens when you are the happiest." I felt such a relief. Some part of me had thought that I had to be Mother Teresa and I hated it that I never would be her. Wow, I could just be me and help where I would be happiest.

I cannot stress enough the importance of looking closely at your heart's desire when choosing who or what you volunteer for. According to Buddhist teachings, we are not meant to make ourselves suffer. The Buddhist teachings are a path towards happiness. We do the best work when we are happy. Fourteen-year-old Chris dealt with this issue when his class assignment was to do volunteer work:

> Our class started a service project. Our teacher said to pick an organization and volunteer four hours per week. At first I tried really hard to work at the soup kitchen. I went every week and served meals, but the harder I worked, the more frustrated I got. You see, I wasn't really cut out to work with the homeless and I felt so guilty that I didn't like it. I finally spoke with my teacher who said, "Try something else, what's your secret dream?" And I thought about it and my real dream had always been to run a youth radio station. So I interned at the news department of the local station and I loved it!

A volunteer center in your town or in your school is an excellent place to find resources. You can search your local newspaper or web sites that list organizations and contact information (at the back of the book, I have listed a few web sites for teens wanting to volunteer). You can also research the kinds of organizations that could use your help, as well as what type of work would be available for someone your age, and what are the needs within your community. Finding out what the community needs is very important rather than imposing your own agenda. We can have all sorts of good intentions and ideas about how we can help, but it is not fair to assume just because we want to do it, it will help the community. Ask and investigate first!

do it together

I find it very helpful to work for change in the world in the company of others. That is why the BASE programs have been so inspiring. Every year a group of ten people create a minicommunity. Each person in the group works with dying people in hospices or in an environmental organization, or in a soup kitchen or homeless shelter. The group members support each other when the daily work gets rough, when someone burns out, or when the work feels hopeless. They also celebrate the victories together. BASE members recognize the importance of community, and a few people even moved into a house together in San Francisco, dedicated to Buddhism and social change!

If you are planning to begin a service project or work for social change, I recommend finding others to do it with you. There may be a service club in your school, or you can invite a group of friends or even family members to join you in an activity such as going to a march or demonstration or cooking at a soup kitchen. There are also service organizations you can join either locally, or national groups where you can spend a few weeks in a program, working on envirmonental or social issues, sometimes even traveling somewhere in need. One friend of mine went to Colombia with fifteen others on a delegation for peace. Social engagement requires the support of friends.

Ultimately we are all helping each other. When seeking a place to serve, you want to strike a balance between what will serve you and what will serve others. This is not selfish, although it might sound that way. From a Buddhist perspective, serving is an opportunity to be helped as much as being served is. Joanna Macy said to me, when I was first developing the BASE program, that we need to be careful not to say we are "serving someone," because in fact, they are also serving us! In the process of serving, we learn more about ourselves—everything from how we react to suffering, to how we find calm amidst intense situa-

wide awake

tions—which is an incredible gift to us. It is much better, Joanna explained, to say that we are "engaging together."

Ultimately the fruit of socially engaged Buddhism is a meaningful life. It is a life where our highest spiritual and social ideals are completely merged. Socially engaged Buddhism invites us to step into our power, to take hold of our inner wisdom that we have developed in our spiritual lives and bring it forward to all who need it. And in the process, we will develop ourselves even more as spiritual beings. We live in a time of great challenges. Who but us will work towards the healing of the planet? One Hopi Elder said, "We are the ones we are waiting for."

exercise: bodhisattva motivation

Here are two practices to develop our Ordinary Bodhisattva motivation.

1. Setting Your Motivation:
If you wish, you can get in touch with a broader intention for your meditation practice. You can develop a motivation where your personal practice benefits not only you, but expands so that as you develop spiritually, you will serve and be useful to others. When you sit down to meditate, you can begin with a wish or prayer, or an expression of good will for others. One traditional expression is "May my meditation practice be a cause for the ending of suffering everywhere." Or, you can use your own words, like, "May my meditation help me to let go of self-centeredness so I can serve others."

Other traditional phrases that you can experiment with are:

✳ For as long as space exists and sentient beings remain, may I be the living ground of love for all beings. (Santideva, 7th century Buddhist saint)

✳ May the awakened heart and mind arise where it has not arisen, and where it has arisen may it not decrease, but increase further and further. (Tibetan Bodhicitta Prayer)

2. Dedicating The Merit:

At the end of your meditation, you might "dedicate the merit," or share all the goodness and beneficial results that come from meditating. You do this so the benefits are not for you alone, but shared with beings everywhere—humans, animals, or the planet itself. You might particularly want to dedicate the merit of your meditation to people you know who are having a hard time—friends, relatives, or people in far away countries in conflict. Some traditional phrases are:

✳ May the merit of my practice penetrate into all things, benefiting all beings in all realms. (Zen dedication)

✳ May the merit of my practice reduce suffering, increase happiness, and result in the awakened heart and mind. (Tibetan prayer)

Note: These two practices are training in opening your heart, and in a sense, building a bridge between your personal spiritual practice and other beings and the earth. It is likely that you will not automatically embody the prayer. Instead, as an Ordinary Bodhisattva, as you say the prayer, the intention develops. You plant a seed inside that brings others and the world more fully into your heart. Try experimenting with the expressions above, or others that may feel more comfortable to you.

twenty

epilogue: commitment

Sometimes I would stand at the edge of my patio
and look out across the mountains and think, "If you
could be anyplace in the whole world, where would
want to be?" And there was nowhere else.
—Ani Tenzin Palmo, a nun who spent
twelve years meditating in a cave

Arriving at the end of a book can feel like the conclusion of a long journey. Perhaps you are worn-out, after all, you have traveled through pages and pages of teachings, stories and concepts. Maybe you are energized. You are left with ideas to assimilate and questions to ponder.

You may have tried some of the practices described in this book. You may have begun meditating, or experimented with some loving-kindness practice. Or maybe you worked on some of the reflections and exercises throughout the book. You could have started to examine behaviors you have done all your life, and even toyed with the idea of taking on a precept or two. Your question might be, where do I go now?

At this point further exploration is up to you. The one thing I am sure of is, your further steps along the Buddhist—or any other spiritual path—is dependent upon one quality: commitment.

People who go to meditate in monasteries in Asia take vows. One might take commitments for many years, such as the vow not to eat after noon, or to be celibate. For shorter periods we might pledge to sit still without moving for one hour or longer. We make these commitments not because we are being forced to follow rules, but because we choose to, because we know of the benefit of commitment. We are curious what making an effort, and pushing ourselves further than we might ordinarily feel comfortable with, will teach us.

A person who commits to an act does so with wholehearted intention to regularly follow or go more fully into that action. Commitment is a quality of the heart—a desire and willingness to try, and to keep trying.

I am not suggesting you become a Buddhist. Buddhists are not known for trying to convert people. What I am recommending is that if you wish to grow spiritually, the best way to begin is to commit. Your commitment can be of any sort: a vow to meditate every day for five minutes, a commitment to speak truthfully for the next month, a promise to attend a meditation retreat some time this coming year. Don't pick something too difficult or you may give up right away. Something too easy is not challenging enough. Experiment until you arrive at the perfect doable, but challenging, commitment. Understanding the teachings of this book requires the simple act of putting one foot forward, consistently over a period of time. If you do this, you will reap results.

In order to make it simple, I would suggest three kinds of commitments you can make in your life: to practice, to love, and to serve. How each one manifests is up to you, but here are a few suggestions:

Practice.
Develop awareness in your life. Sit every day if you resonated with it. If you prefer to be active, bring awareness into your walking meditation or movement or any activity that you do. Be-

come aware of your body, thoughts, emotions, mind, reactions, motivations, and joys. Wake up!

Love:
Love yourself. Trust in your inner goodness. Don't be too heavy on yourself, keep a sense of humor. Love the people in your life. Love them by acting in harmonious ways, by bringing awareness to your behavior, by acting with integrity. Love the world.

Serve:
Work for change. Help other beings who need it. Take care of the planet, take care of your neighborhood. Fully be yourself and bring yourself into the world in the spirit of service.

These are my suggestions. And remember, don't take my word for it. The Buddha encourages us to be wise. With any teaching, remember, he recommended that you examine it closely to see if it makes sense in light of your direct experience and best intelligence.

So, make a commitment, observe the results over time, and if you find out for yourself that it leads to happiness, then continue, if not, stop doing it. Are you happier? How are people around you? Keep in mind, there is no way forward without trying, without commitment, no matter how small. Commit to practice, to love, and to serve, and see what happens in your life. You can wake up in any moment, or even in all moments, all you have to do is try.

May this book be a cause for the liberation of all beings, reducing suffering, increasing happiness, and engendering the awakened heart and mind!

appendices

glossary

anatta—(Pali) not self, no permanent, fixed identity

anicca—(Pali) impermanence, change

ascetic—one who does severe religious practices such as fasting or standing on one foot for long periods of time

Buddha—the Awakened One, Siddhartha Gautama, the Prince who "woke up"

Bodhisattva—(Sanskrit) one who chooses to become enlightened for the sake of all beings

dharma—(Sanskrit) the Truth, Natural Law, the way things are, and, most commonly, the Teachings of the Buddha

disidentify—to not believe something you think or feel so strongly, nor take it to be truth about yourself

dukkha—(Pali) suffering, unsatisfactoriness

enlightenment—fully waking up, the cessation of suffering

ethics—morals, values by which we live

guru—(Sanskrit) a teacher, commonly a spiritual teacher

kalyana mitta—(Pali) a spiritual friend, originally the Buddha himself. More commonly, someone who is a guide and companion on the spiritual path karma—(Sanskrit) a word meaning action, generally known as the law of cause and effect

lay people—the traditional word for people who are not monks or nuns and follow a spiritual path

livelihood—how one makes a living

mantra—(Sanskrit) a sacred word one can repeat to gain concentration or to remind oneself of some truth

Mara—(Pali) The God of Temptation, equivalent to the Buddhist devil

metta—(Pali) lovingkindness: the wish for all beings to be happy and free from all suffering

mindfulness—a quality of mind that stays connected to and aware of whatever is happening. It does not forget whatever is present

monasticism—living in a monastery as a monk or nun

noble—a translation of the Pali word *ariya*, which means beyond the reach of internal enemies that disturb our lives. Used here as in Four Noble Truths

nirvana—(Sanskrit) the cessation of suffering, the highest peace

Pali—the language of the Early Buddhist texts or scriptures

precept—a guide for making moral choices, ethical guideline

right—in the Buddhist context means that which leads to freedom from suffering. As in "right speech." Wrong would be that which leads away from freedom, to more suffering

sangha—(Pali) the community of followers of the Buddha, also any community of Buddhist practitioners

Sanskrit—the sacred and literary language of ancient India

skillful—in the Buddhist context means leads to harmony and prevents suffering

sutta—(Pali) a teaching, a Buddhist scripture

glossary

vipassana—(Pali) insight into the nature of things. A kind of meditation practice

zafu—a round cushion used for sitting meditation, originally from Japan

Zen—a school of Japanese Buddhism, popular in the West

suggested reading

Boorstein, Sylvia. *It's Easier Than You Think: The Buddhist Way to Happiness*. San Francisco: HarperSanFrancisco, 1995.

Chodron, Pema. *Start Where You Are: A Guide to Compassionate Living*. Boston: Shambhala Publications, 2001.

Fischer, Norman. *Taking Our Places: The Buddhist Path of Truly Growing Up*. San Francisco: HarperSanFrancisco, 2003. (This book is on Buddhism and mentoring youth).

Goldstein, Joseph. *The Experience of Insight: A Simple and Direct Guide to Buddhist Meditation*. Boston: Shambhala Publishers, 1987.

Gordhamer, Soren. *Just Say Om!: Your Life's Journey*. Adams Media Corporation, 2001. (This book is written for teenagers, and is about the spiritual journey).

His Holiness the Dalai Lama. *Freedom in Exile: The Autobiography of the Dalai Lama*. New York: Harper Perrenial, 1990.

Jackson, Phil. *Sacred Hoops: Spiritual Lessons of a Hardwood Warrior*. New York: Hyperion, 1996.

Kornfield, Jack. *A Path with a Heart: A Guide through the Perils and Promises of Spiritual Life*. New York: Bantam Books, 1993.

Kraft, Kenneth. *The Wheel of Engaged Buddhism: A New Map of the Path*. New York: Weatherhill, 2000.

Lama Surya Das. *Awakening the Buddha Within*. New York: Broadway Books, 1997.

Levine, Noah. *Dharma Punx*. San Francisco: HarperSanFrancisco, 2003.

Loundon, Sumi, ed. *Blue Jean Buddha: Voices of Young Buddhists*. Boston: Wisdom Publications, 2001.

Maha Ghosananda, *Step by Step*. California: Parallax Press, 1992.

Salzberg, Sharon. *Lovingkindness: The Revolutionary Art of Happiness*. Boston: Shambhala Publications, 1997.

Schmidt, Amy. *Knee Deep in Grace: The Extraordinary Life and Teachings of Dipa Ma*. North Carolina: Present Perfect Books, 2003.

Suzuki, Shunryu. *Zen Mind, Beginner's Mind*. New York: Weatherhill, 1994.

Thich Nhat Hanh. *The Miracle of Mindfulness*. Boston: Beacon Press, 1996.

practice centers

The following retreat centers in the United States offer meditation classes, programs, and retreats for young people:

Insight Meditation Center 1230 Pleasant St. Barre, MA 01005, (978) 355-4378, www.dharma.org (holds a yearly teen retreat).

Spirit Rock Meditation Center P.O. Box 169, Woodacre, CA, 94973, (415) 488-0164, www.spiritrock.org (contact Family and Teen Program).

Shambhala Mountain Center 4921 County Rd 68-C, Red Feather Lakes, CO 80545, (970) 881-2184, www.shambhalamountain.org

San Francisco Zen Center 300 Page Street San Francisco, CA 94102, (415) 863-3136, www.sfzc.org (has coming-of-age programs for 12–15 year olds).

Green Gulch Farm 1601 Shoreline Highway, Sausalito, CA 94965, (415) 383-3134, www.sfzc.org/ggfindex.htm

Naropa University 2130 Arapahoe Ave. Boulder, CO, 80302, (303) 444-0202, www.naropa.edu (Buddhist university with undergraduate degree program).

For more information on socially engaged Buddhism and BASE: Buddhist Peace Fellowship, P.O. Box 4650 Berkeley, CA 94704 (510)655-6169 www.bpf.org

Some web sites that offer helpful information for youth about volunteerism include: www.pitchin.org

www.serviceleader.org/advice/youth.html

www.ala.org/teenhoopla/activism.html

For further information on Buddhism and teenagers, to give feedback, participate in online discussions, to contact the author, and for schedule of retreats, classes, and events, go to: www.wide-awake.org

practice centers

index

index

index

Credit: Martin Matzinger

I n 1988, Diana Winston graduated from Brown University and flew to Asia, where she encountered Buddhism. She quickly realized she had found her spiritual home. Since then, she has studied and practiced meditation with many extraordinary teachers including: The Dalai Lama, Thich Nhat Hanh, Sayadaw U Pandita, Joseph Goldstein, Michele McDonald-Smith, Tsoknyi Rinpoche, and Joanna Macy, among others. Her main practice is insight meditation or vipassanā. In 1998, she was ordained as a Buddhist nun, shaved her head, and spent a year meditating in a Burmese monastery. Today she is no longer a nun, but lives in Berkeley, California, where she practices meditation, teaches meditation to youth and adults, and works as a spiritual activist and writer. She has taught and lectured nationally on socially engaged Buddhism—the intersection of Buddhism with progressive social change. She is the founder of the Buddhist Alliance for Social Engagement (BASE), and the former associate director of the Buddhist Peace Fellowship. Her website is www.wide-awake.org.